Buy A Cabin
The Theology and Practice of Rest

Robert L. Franck

BUY A CABIN: The Theology and Practice of Rest

Library of Congress Control Number: 2015919959
CreateSpace Independent Publishing Platform, North Charleston, SC

ISBN-10: 1519384580

ISBN-13: 978-1519384584

For Lori

My perfect match, by God's insight.
She tends to all, I sit and write.

Rest is the least taught subject in Christendom.

On those occasions when it is mentioned,
rest becomes the worst taught subject.

Contents

Introduction 1

PART I—The Theology of Rest

1. In God's Image 7
2. What Is Work? 11
3. The Purpose of Rest 16
4. WDJD—What Did Jesus Do? 18
5. Rest Freedom 26
6. Future Rest 30
7. Take a Deep Breath 39
8. Two Buckets 40
9. Secular Work 46
10. Spiritual Rest 52
11. Worldly Earthly Fleshyness 64
12. Theology Complete 72

PART II—The Practical Theory of Rest

13. Painting with Mr. Churchill 75
14. Unconcentrating 87
15. No Time for Rest? 96
16. What Am I Doing Under the Cabin? 107
17. The Fellowship of the Exhausted 115
18. Idleness Revisited 124
19. Structure 132
20. The Rest-O-Meter 140
21. Resting with God 149
22. Lower Your Expectations 155

PART III—The Experience of Rest

23. Reading for Pleasure 163
24. Get in the Game 173
25. Going Somewhere Else 177
26. Roughing It 188
27. The Cabin 193
28. Everything Else 199

Final Thought: Something To Look Forward To 201

Appendix A: Your Theological Jigsaw Puzzle 203

Introduction

I bought a cabin.

There are reasons *not* to buy a cabin. I know them well. They all boil down to this: A cabin is ultimately a waste of time and money. But let's unboil these reasons—ponder them—for a moment. Money first.

A Waste of Money

The first objection to buying a cabin is that you cannot afford to buy one. If you cannot afford to buy a cabin, you should not buy one. That is clear enough and unarguable. But I am not the "you" here. I can afford to buy a cabin. Somehow—through no great planning on my part—I discovered myself in the middle class. This has been a surprise to me and, I have found, a burden. Life was much simpler when I was poorer. Excess money used to be what I set aside so that I could buy the next set of tires. Now, in my opulence, I can buy the next set of tires and I still have money left over. Uh-oh! More responsibility. This leads to....

The second objection to buying a cabin is that you *should not* buy one. Why not? Because you—and I—have better things to do with our money. In economic terms this is known as "opportunity cost." Opportunity cost is the comparative value of alternatives. I can invest in a cabin or I can invest in a missions project or in a university education for my children or in the building program at church or in a sports car or in alleviating hunger or in travel. Which is the best use of my money? In biblical terms opportunity cost is known as "stewardship." We are to make the most of what God provides for us. And all things are to glorify Him and further His kingdom.

In God's economy isn't there always a better opportunity cost alternative than buying a cabin? Isn't cabin buying lousy stewardship? Surely donating that excess money to missions work, for example, builds God's kingdom more than a cabin ever could. The first is selfless, the second is selfish. Missions is Christ centered, the cabin is me centered. And besides, the cabin is so…so…middle class-ish.

Isn't true, vibrant Christianity antithetical to the middle-class lifestyle, such as cabins? Weren't the Pharisees middle class? We suspect that if anyone had cabins in Palestine, it would have been the Pharisees—stealing widows' mites so that they would have a place to display the heads of their trophy stags.

I have perused some books my son has bought recently. It is easy to catch their gist:

> *trade in their false American dreams*
> *radical discipleship*
> *break free from the status quo*
> *awaken a church mired in the middle ground*

Are they talking about me—the comfortable middle-class guy with the cabin? I think so. These are just like the books I read when I was my son's age. I thought the same thoughts. *The church has gotten soft, weak, materialistic, traditionalistic, inbred, irrelevant and isolated. The church needs whole-hearted, sold-out warriors that are willing to risk all, give all and hold nothing back for the sake of the Gospel! This includes money. I will give away all I have, except the minimum needed to sustain a frugal and humble life. I will not become complacent like those worn-out old saints that wear ties and flower print dresses and drive nice cars…and have cabins.* My commitment to give away all in excess of a frugal and humble life was a real one, but I did not have much to give away because a frugal and humble life was all I could then sustain. It also did not dawn on me that those people with the cars and cabins were bankrolling most of the kingdom work.

Nevertheless, it is a privilege of youth to be idealistic. To be idealistic in pursuit of God's glory is a noble thing indeed, and I am glad to see it in my son. Have I betrayed that idealism that was in me as well? I never would have considered buying a cabin thirty years ago, even if I could have afforded one. Have I lost my fire? Am I saltless, backsliding, lukewarm? I—Cabin Man.

But it gets worse.

A Waste of Time

Jesus specifically instructs about money investment in his parables (Matthew 25, Luke 19), but does he care about how we spend our time?

INTRODUCTION

Does God hold us accountable for the stewardship of dollars but not minutes? Is Christian living only about the wallet and not the watch? I think not. For one thing, the money parables end in eternal judgment. Salvation is surely not only for the savvy investor. A bad stock pick will not automatically lead to damnation. The point of the money parables seems to be that the faithful provide a good return to the Master from all that he has entrusted to them. Paul—also in the context of eternal judgment—expounds on this understanding when he commands Christians to live wisely, "making the best use of the time (Ephesians 5:16)." Stewardship applies to all of life and, as Benjamin Franklin noted, time "is the stuff life is made of."

So, not content to only be a squanderer of my money on the cabin, have I also been a wastrel with my time? Well, perhaps so. Come to the cabin and make your own judgment.

My cabin is in the mountains of Colorado. It takes me about an hour and a half to drive there. A round trip costs three hours of time. *Ka-ching* (this is the sound of an ancient cash register). Write three hours under expenditures in the ledger. Now for the main investment—time actually spent at the cabin. This will range from one to nine days or, if you prefer, from sixteen to 216 hours. *Ka-ching.* Let's categorize this further. First, there is cabin maintenance. So far my time cost in cabin maintenance has been extensive…to say the least. The cabin is forty years old and had been neglected for the last twenty. It required attention. *Ka-ching.* More about this later. Second, there is the other time at the cabin—the point of having a cabin. I'll label this time as "goofing off" because that is what you probably think it is at this point. Goofing off expenditure. The biggest ticket item. *Ka-ching-a-ling!*

There is opportunity cost for time just as there is for money. What is the opportunity cost here? Instead of spending all of that time on cabin maintenance and goofing off, I could have invested in alternatives—evangelizing my neighbors, writing this book, earning more money, ladling soup at the city mission, or in prayer and Bible study, for instance. Surely some alternatives would have been more beneficial to the kingdom. What have I done? Miserable steward that I am!

Aren't Christians supposed to forsake this world, earthly things, materialism, ease, distractions, amusements…cabins! Aren't we in a cosmic battle where eternity is at stake for each person—heaven or hell? On top of that we have all of the pressing problems of living in this fallen world—death, suffering, pain, poverty, war, terrorism, displacement, financial collapse, unemployment, politics, pandemics, starvation, injustice. In light of this, who has time and money for a cabin?

Well…I do.

I do because I value rest. And a cabin is all about rest.

Neglect and Error

Rest is the least taught subject in Christendom. When was the last time you heard a sermon on rest? When have you read a book on rest (besides this one)? Considering that about half of your time is spent on rest, this is odd. You would think that such a large proportion of life would warrant more attention. After all, you believe that Jesus is Lord of *all*, don't you? He is not just Lord of some little private sphere or certain good works. No. He is Lord of everything, everywhere, every moment. If so, then rest should be an area of attention and emphasis.

On those occasions when it is addressed, rest transitions from being the least taught subject in Christendom to being the worst taught subject in Christendom. The root of this confusion is the failure to make proper distinctions. Rest is not work. Rest is not idleness. Rest is not optional. Rest is not "unspiritual." And rest is not specified under the New Covenant as it was under the Old Covenant.

On the positive side, rest is a blessing from God. Rest is a means to glorify God. Rest is a multiplier of work. Rest is good in and of itself.

I hope to persuade you of these things.

This book begins with a survey of the biblical teaching on rest, starting in Genesis, with the creation, and ending in Revelation, with the new creation. I also explore the pervasive errors that hinder many Christians from resting well. Once this foundation is laid, I move to practical considerations in the final two sections of the book. I make some observations about the nature of rest, which describe its characteristics and dynamics. Then I provide a few examples from my own experience. These bring together all that has gone before, illustrating both the theology and theory of rest.

And I talk about my cabin along the way.

PART I

The Theology of Rest

The Creator God surely knows what's best.
He worked a while and then took a rest.

He made a man and said, "You've work to do."
The man replied, "Yes, Lord. I know that's true."

Then God asked, "After work, what should be?"
The man pondered and said, "It's beyond me."

God asked once more, "Can't you see what is clear?"
"Oh, Lord!" said man, "This is an issue here!"

So man missed the obvious and gave hard thought.
And tied up his theology into a pretzel knot.

But theology's not the problem, it is the key.
Understanding the Bible will set rest free.

Brace yourself, friend. Brain power is required ahead.
Do this work, lest you work yourself dead.

CHAPTER ONE

In God's Image

Protestants are distinguished by our debates over doctrine. So many interpretations of the Bible! So much bickering! This seems like the worst situation imaginable...except for the alternative.

Whether you like it or not, debate is necessary. It is the means by which truth is clarified and error is exposed. The New Testament, you may have observed, is full of debate. The first section of this book is my contribution to this honorable tradition.

Sometimes the debate involves the fundamentals of the faith. *Who is Jesus? What is the relationship between faith and works? Are there "many paths" to God?* These are not disagreements among those within the faith but are disputes with those who have left the faith. Usually the path away from faith begins with rejection of the reliability and authority of the Bible, which is the fundamental of the faith that defines the fundamentals of the faith. Once this foundation is abandoned nothing remains of historic Christianity for long, except perhaps the trappings—old buildings, religious talk and symbolic rituals and clothing. But unbelief dressed in vestments is still unbelief. Debate over the fundamentals of the faith is not an iron-sharpens-iron type of debate. There must be no compromise with apostasy.

But the debate that this book encourages is for those who respect the Bible and submit to it. We agree on the standard. It's just some of the details that we see differently. In fact, we squabble over a hundred things. *How are the spiritual gifts to be expressed? What is the right form of church government? How is man's responsibility reconciled with God's sovereignty?* These are not trivial matters. They shape the understanding and practice of faith. And because they are important, you and I should wrestle over them in order to arrive at a better grasp of truth.

Rest is one of these matters.

A "within the family" debate over such a topic is never easy. Why? Because the Bible is a complex book and you interpret it within a larger framework. This is your theology—a logical understanding of how the teachings in the Bible fit together. You probably inherited your theology from the tradition you grew up with. Or you may have switched traditions because you became convinced that another theological approach more accurately reflected biblical teaching. In either case, your theological system shapes the way you interpret the biblical text. [1]

And this is why you are confused about rest.

What follows is my attempt to outline a consistent and, more importantly, scripturally faithful theology of rest. Feel free to challenge it. This is your responsibility. Whether or not you agree completely with me, my hope is that you will gain a more biblical understanding of rest.

I will begin at the beginning.

God Rests, Man Rests

The first chapters of Genesis provide the basis for understanding both God and man. All subsequent teaching is built upon what we learn here. And here is rest:

> And on the seventh day God finished his work that he had done, and he rested on the seventh day from all his work that he had done. So God blessed the seventh day and made it holy, because on it God rested from all his work that he had done in creation.
>
> Genesis 2:2-3

This passage is so familiar that we miss the shock and significance of the revelation that God, the Almighty Creator who spoke the universe into existence, rested! This is not a detail that we would anticipate. These verses contain the first use of the word *rest* in the

---

[1] See Appendix A, *Your Theological Jigsaw Puzzle*, for a more complete description of how your theology is formed and adjusted.

Bible, which follows the first use of the word *work*. God worked and then he rested. First work, second rest. He rested because he worked. These two activities are inseparable. One leads to the other.

God made man in his image as the final and crowning work of creation. Because God works, he created man "to work [the garden] and keep it" (Genesis 2:15). This was not an afterthought for God. *Now that I've made him, I better keep him busy or he'll get into trouble.* No. Man, as the image bearer of God, was created for work. Adam's wife, Eve, was created to help him accomplish this work. Together, male and female, they were to fulfill God's mandate to "be fruitful and multiply and fill the earth and subdue it and have dominion" over the animals (Genesis1:28).

But unlike God's rest, there is no reference to man's rest in the creation account. If God works and rests, shouldn't man also rest after he works? As we move to the second book of the Bible we find the answer to this question. What is implied in Genesis is described in Exodus:

> Remember the Sabbath day, to keep it holy. Six days you shall labor, and do all your work, but the seventh day is a Sabbath to the LORD your God. On it you shall not do any work, you, or your son, or your daughter, your male servant, or your female servant, or your livestock, or the sojourner who is within your gates. For in six days the LORD made heaven and earth, the sea, and all that is in them, and rested on the seventh day. Therefore the LORD blessed the Sabbath day and made it holy.
>
> Exodus 20:8-11

You will recognize this passage as the fourth of the Ten Commandments. The Ten Commandments, which are part of a larger body of law given through Moses, contained the terms of the covenant that God established with the nation of Israel. This law, known as the Mosaic Law, required a very specific practice of rest on the Sabbath. I will examine the relationship of the Mosaic Law to Christians shortly, but for now I only draw a general principle concerning rest from this text. *All* were to rest—servants, sojourners, even livestock—not just the Jews. All were to rest because God, the Creator, rests. Not only were all creatures to rest but even the land was to rest, as we learn in Exodus 23:10-11: "For six years you shall sow your land and gather in its yield, but the seventh year you shall let it rest and lie fallow...." God rested and, therefore, all of his creation—man, animals, land—is to rest.

What is Rest?

So there is a created order. Work is followed by rest. But *what* is rest? It is time to define the word. The Genesis passage above says that God "finished his work" and rested "from all his work." How does God rest? He does not work. He ceases from his work.

Is this concept of rest—a ceasing of work—also true for man? Yes, it is. The phrase "not do any work" or a variation is repeated over and over again in reference to the Sabbath, as cited in the fourth commandment above. But the seventh day was not the only time work was prohibited. The Day of Atonement, which is called a "Sabbath of rest," the Passover, and the ceremonial feasts were also times of "no ordinary work." All of these were holy days, that is, days that were set apart. Set apart from what? Answer: from work. Days that are not for work are for rest. Therefore, the biblical definition of rest is simply not-work.

Excuse me.

Yes, reader.

May I ask a question.

Of course. Jump in at any time.

Which of my activities should be classified as work and which should be classified as rest?

Here is the rub: the Scripture never defines the activities that are classified as rest. Rest is only defined negatively, rest is not-work, rather than positively, rest is _____. Am I stuck? Must I end this investigation of rest? Thankfully not. Although I cannot identify actions that belong in the category of rest, I can find a good description of work in the Bible.

CHAPTER TWO

What is Work?

Take another look at Genesis. Just after God commanded man to fill, subdue and rule the earth—the Dominion Mandate or, more simply, the Work Mandate—is the first mention of food:

> And God said, "Behold, I have given you every plant
> yielding seed that is on the face of all the earth, and every
> tree with seed in its fruit. You shall have them for food."
> Genesis 1:29

Food is connected to work. The purpose of work is to produce food. Man works in order to eat. Because he works, he may partake of the fruit of his labor. We commonly use the phrase "earning his bread" in reference to work. This is a biblical concept.

The Jews would not have missed the linkage between work and food.

> On the sixth day they gathered twice as much bread, two
> omers each. And when all the leaders of the congregation
> came and told Moses, he said to them, "This is what the
> LORD has commanded: 'Tomorrow is a day of solemn
> rest, a holy Sabbath to the LORD; bake what you will bake
> and boil what you will boil, and all that is left over lay aside
> to be kept till the morning.'"
> Exodus 16:22-23

Food, work and rest are all in this passage. The Israelites in the wilderness were instructed to collect and prepare enough bread, or manna, each day to sustain them. This was their work. The exception was on the sixth day when they were to prepare twice as much manna, so that they would not need to work on the seventh day, the day of rest. Because work was prohibited on the Sabbath, the Israelites could not gather, bake or boil manna on that day. They could eat their bread, of course, but they were prohibited from earning it. That would be a violation of Sabbath rest.

Even in ancient societies not everyone's livelihood always involved direct food production. In Numbers chapter fifteen a man was caught gathering sticks on the Sabbath. Gathering sticks was work, a violation of the Sabbath. In Nehemiah chapter thirteen men were engaging in commerce on the Sabbath. This was work, a "desecration" of Sabbath rest. Work is whatever one does to earn his bread.

In our day, we often equate work with pay. But this limits the definition of work too much. We may get paid for some work and do not get paid for other work. The homemaker is certainly working but receives no salary for this work. She deserves to eat. As for her husband, he is getting paid while "on the clock," but he may need to do some uncompensated work when he gets home, such as fix the leak under the sink or discipline Junior for talking back to his mother. As for Junior, his work at this stage in his life is his schooling, which is preparation for future work, as well as doing some chores. And in fifty years when Junior grows old and retires, he will still have plenty of work to do in order to sustain life. Just as in the Old Testament, everyone should work to provide for themselves and their families.

Sharing and Gleaning

Here is another aspect of work.

> Let the thief no longer steal, but rather let him labor, doing honest work with his own hands, so that he may have something to share with anyone in need.
> Ephesians 4:28

The thief's work is to steal the fruit of others' work. This is sinful work and, if he is to love and serve Jesus, the thief must change his profession and get a different job. But his new labor should not only

12

produce enough to support himself but also some excess that can be shared with others. In relation to work, Jesus changes a man from a taker to a giver. In addition to yourselves and your families, your work is to provide sustenance for others in need.

"Others in need" are those who because of some misfortune or inability cannot fully earn their own bread. You are to love them by providing for them. Still you must be careful not to rob them of the dignity of working to the extent that they are able. A fitting picture is the Old Testament requirement not to harvest the edges of the field or the gleanings (Leviticus 23:22). This was to be left for the needy that could come and harvest enough for themselves, as Boaz allowed Ruth to do. Here was a balance of gracious provision for the disadvantaged and work according to their ability.

Ministry is Work

Here is a final aspect of work.

> Now if anyone builds on the foundation with gold, silver, precious stones, wood, hay, straw—each one's work will become manifest, for the Day will disclose it, because it will be revealed by fire, and the fire will test what sort of work each one has done. If the work that anyone has built on the foundation survives, he will receive a reward.
> I Corinthians 3:13-14

All Christians, not just those in paid service, are to use their gifts and abilities to build Christ's Church. This is work. The pastor is working when he is preaching Sunday morning, as are the Sunday school teachers, the worship team, and those who are swabbing babies' bottoms in the nursery. Outreach ministry, such as missions, church planting and evangelism, are work, as well as efforts that display Christ through what we fittingly call "good works." Christian ministry is work.

You have a responsibility to work in all the ways identified above— earning your bread, sharing what you earn, and ministering to others. In each case, work provides for a need, either your own need or someone else's.

Based on all of this, at long last, here is a definition of work:

Activities that provide for your needs,
your family's needs and the needs of others.

Sluggards, Shirkers and Slackers

Hello! It's me again—your reader. I have another question. So you are saying that
when I am providing for needs I am working…and everything else I do is rest. Is
that your point?

Yes…but there is an exception. Let me introduce another concept
now. The Bible calls it "idleness." Idleness is always condemned. In
the Old Testament it is condemned most notably in the "sluggard"
proverbs, such as here:

> As a door turns on its hinges, so does a sluggard on his
> bed.
>> Proverbs 26:14

The sluggard refuses to work. He always has a reason—an excuse—
for not doing it.

> The sluggard says, "There is a lion outside! I shall be
> killed in the streets!"
>> Proverbs 23:13

The sluggard is a wicked fool. His sloth does not merely provide
fodder for good satire. He will suffer grievously for his idleness, and
so will others that depend upon him. Not working is a serious matter.

Wait! You said that "not-work" is the definition for rest. If idleness is "not
working," isn't that the same thing?

No, although they are often confused. The difference is that rest is
ceasing work after you have worked, while idleness is not working in
the first place. Rest is taking a break after you have earned your bread,
while idleness is refusing to earn your bread.

The Apostle Paul weighs in on the subject here:

Now we command you, brothers, in the name of our Lord
Jesus Christ, that you keep away from any brother who is
walking in idleness and not in accord with the tradition
that you received from us. For you yourselves know how
you ought to imitate us, because we were not idle when we
were with you, nor did we eat anyone's bread without
paying for it, but with toil and labor we worked night and
day, that we might not be a burden to any of you. It was
not because we do not have that right, but to give you in
ourselves an example to imitate. For even when we were
with you, we would give you this command: If anyone is
not willing to work, let him not eat. For we hear that some
among you walk in idleness, not busy at work, but
busybodies. Now such persons we command and
encourage in the Lord Jesus Christ to do their work quietly
and to earn their own living.

II Thessalonians 3:6-12

Besides contrasting work and idleness, Paul repeats the biblical
connection between working and eating. If the idler is not willing to
work, he should not eat. He should be shunned by the church until he
repents of his sin.

So then, the sluggard, the idler, is not condemned for resting. He is
condemned for refusing to work. It is, in fact, impossible for the idler
to rest from his work when he has not worked in the first place. The
created order is work *then* rest. The sluggard cannot enjoy the cream
because he does not milk the cow.

I will revisit this topic in the next section of this book. But now I
have a question for you. "*Why* do you rest?"

CHAPTER THREE

The Purpose of Rest

Now that you know what work is, you know what rest is not. Also, you know that rest is not idleness. All of these negatives! Isn't there some positive way to define rest? Yes, there is. The purpose of rest—the *why* of rest—reveals what rest is.

Let us return to Exodus.

> ...in six days the LORD made heaven and earth, and on the seventh day he rested and was refreshed.
>
> Exodus 31:17

As before, you must first learn about God before you can understand yourself. Why does God rest? Because rest *refreshed* God. This is as astounding as the fact that God rested at all! Now what about you? What is the purpose of your rest?

> Six days you shall do your work, but on the seventh day you shall rest; that your ox and your donkey may have rest, and the son of your servant woman, and the alien, may be refreshed.
>
> Exodus 23:12

Just as the Creator is refreshed by rest, so man, made in his image, is refreshed by rest. The Hebrew word—translated as "refreshed" in these passages—is *nāphash*. It means "to breathe" or "to take breath." When someone has greatly exerted himself we use the expression: *Take a breather.* At face value this seems nonsensical because a person must breathe or die. But we all understand what is meant: catch your breath, relax, recover. There is also a figurative sense to *nāphash*. It is to be refreshed "as if by a current of air." This too is easy to grasp. Recall a time when you were working on a hot day and a cool breeze blew across you. Refreshment!

Even without the Hebrew lesson the meaning is clear enough from the context of these passages. Work is followed by rest. Rest provides respite, renewal and rejuvenation.

With this understanding, I am able to define what rest is.

Activities that refresh you after you have provided
for the needs of yourself, your family and others.

The definition is accurate but not concise enough to remember. I will reduce the description of rest down to the term itself.

Activities that refresh you after your work.

Simple enough?

CHAPTER FOUR

WDJD – WHAT DID JESUS DO?

So far I have explored the "what" and "why" of rest but not the "when" of rest. When do Christians rest? Because the "when" of rest was mandated for the Jews under the Old Covenant and because it is not specifically commanded for Christians under the New Covenant, this has proven to be a difficult and controversial question.

But we can learn from the Master on this subject. Jesus fulfills the Old Covenant and inaugurates the New. He teaches us both by word and deed.

Think Like a Pharisee

When I read the gospels I attempt to mentally adopt the cultural mindset of first century Palestine. That is, I try to think like the Jews of that day. If you have read the Old Testament—the Old Covenant— this seems straightforward. Obedience to the terms of the covenant, as defined by Mosaic Law, brought blessing. Disobedience to the covenant brought cursing. Because the nation of Israel violated the terms of the covenant, the whole nation suffered the curses of the covenant in the dispersion and by political oppression of Rome. The Jews strove to regain God's blessing and liberation through zealous obedience to the Law, both in as written by Moses, the Torah, and its oral tradition, as championed by the Pharisees. If I had been born a Jew in Jesus' day, I'm pretty sure that I would have agreed with this rigorous law keeping. After all, what could be more important than keeping God's commandments to obtain his blessings? I may have even become a committed Pharisee, like Saul.

Much of the focus of law obedience concerned rest, that is, Sabbath observance. There was a biblical basis for this, of course.

> And the LORD said to Moses, "You are to speak to the
> people of Israel and say, 'Above all you shall keep my
> Sabbaths, for this is a sign between me and you
> throughout your generations, that you may know that I,
> the LORD, sanctify you. You shall keep the Sabbath,
> because it is holy for you. Everyone who profanes it shall
> be put to death. Whoever does any work on it, that soul
> shall be cut off from among his people. Six days shall work
> be done, but the seventh day is a Sabbath of solemn rest,
> holy to the LORD. Whoever does any work on the Sabbath
> day shall be put to death. Therefore the people of Israel
> shall keep the Sabbath, observing the Sabbath throughout
> their generations, as a covenant forever. It is a sign forever
> between me and the people of Israel that in six days the
> LORD made heaven and earth, and on the seventh day he
> rested and was refreshed.'"
>
> Exodus 31:12-17

I have cited the last sentence previously. You should like the part about being refreshed by rest. As for the beginning of the passage, you should be thankful that this is not the covenant that God made with Christians! If it was, you would be obligated to refrain from working on the Sabbath just as the Jews were. Violation would result in death! Twice in the passage the Sabbath is called a "sign." A sign of what? A sign that the working-resting God had set Israel apart through a special relationship with himself. For the Jews then, Sabbath observance was covenantal obedience.

You may be quick to condemn the Jews of Jesus' day for their "legalistic" interpretation of the Mosaic Law. *They were so foolish and missed the point!* Really? Read the passage above from Exodus chapter thirty-one again. Do you understand the point? Sabbath violation = covenant breaking = death. The covenant breaker's death protected Israel from national covenant breaking, which would result in national cursing. Law obedience was serious business.

You should not criticize the Jews for being obsessed with law keeping when life and death was at stake. You should also not criticize them for their preoccupation with extrapolations of the oral Law. You take our own laws seriously, especially whenever you must defend your life or your fortune. You don't hire a lawyer and tell him, "Hey! Don't fixate on all of the little details and precedents." You want him to fixate and are willing to pay him a basketful of money for his effort.

Here then is a summary of the Jews' position.

Covenant	Covenant People	Practice of Rest	Principle
Old or Mosaic	Israel	Observe Sabbath regulations…very carefully!	Obedience/disobedience results in blessing/cursing.

The Jews institutionalized this understanding in their traditions, as was expressed by Tevye, the milkman, practical philosopher and aspiring rabbi in the musical *The Fiddler on the Roof*: "Because of our traditions, every one of us knows who he is and what God expects him to do."

Shake It Up!

Jesus challenged these traditions when he said, "Do not think that I have come to abolish the Law or the Prophets; I have not come to abolish them but to fulfill them" (Matthew. 5:19). He taught that fulfilling the Law involved more than external obedience to the letter of the Law. Jesus required heart obedience to the spirit of the Law, which he called "the weightier matters of the law: justice and mercy and faithfulness" (Matthew 23:23).

This proved controversial, which was evident by the violent reaction of many of the Jewish leaders. He threatened—they thought—their religion, their authority, and their nation with his teaching. Other provocateurs had raised themselves up during those turbulent times, but the difference was that this man, Jesus, performed undeniable miracles that provided him the credentials of a prophet of God.

I will examine two pivotal passages concerning his teaching on rest, one from the first gospel and the other from the last.

At that time Jesus went through the grainfields on the Sabbath. His disciples were hungry, and they began to pluck heads of grain and to eat. But when the Pharisees saw it, they said to him, "Look, your disciples are doing what is not lawful to do on the Sabbath." He said to them, "Have you not read what David did when he was hungry, and those who were with him: how he entered the house of God and ate the bread of the Presence, which it was not lawful for him to eat nor for those who were with him, but only for the priests? Or have you not read in the Law how on the Sabbath the priests in the temple profane the Sabbath and are guiltless? I tell you, something greater than the temple is here. And if you had known what this means, 'I desire mercy, and not sacrifice,' you would not have condemned the guiltless. For the Son of Man is lord of the Sabbath." He went on from there and entered their synagogue. And a man was there with a withered hand. And they asked him, "Is it lawful to heal on the Sabbath?"—so that they might accuse him. He said to them, "Which one of you who has a sheep, if it falls into a pit on the Sabbath, will not take hold of it and lift it out? Of how much more value is a man than a sheep! So it is lawful to do good on the Sabbath." Then he said to the man, "Stretch out your hand." And the man stretched it out, and it was restored, healthy like the other. But the Pharisees went out and conspired against him, how to destroy him.

Matthew 12:1-14

Prior to this confrontation there is clearly tension between the Pharisees and Jesus, but this tension explodes into open conflict right here. Sabbath observance is the detonator. The result is that the Pharisees begin to conspire to kill Jesus, which they eventually accomplished through his crucifixion. What could Jesus have possibly said about *rest* that would trigger such a response?

There are two activities at issue—eating and healing. We will examine them one at a time.

The first forbidden Sabbath activity was plucking grain, which the disciples were doing. The Pharisees pointed out that this was "not lawful." They were right. It was not lawful Sabbath activity under Mosaic Law because plucking grain was work. Jesus did not respond by cleverly manipulating the Law with additional details and qualifications by saying something like this: "Well, my disciples did not technically break the law because merely reaching down and plucking a few heads of grain falls under the threshold of work and, therefore, is not classified as work." This is the way the legalistic Pharisees approached the Sabbath ordinances, but not Jesus. Instead, he agreed that it was "not lawful." He uses these very words to describe David's act, which he cites as a similar deed in relation to the law.

Jesus also points out that the temple priests "profane the Sabbath" by performing their work. All three—disciples, David, priests—violated the Law, yet they were "guiltless." How can this be? To resolve this paradox, Jesus states this principle: "I desire mercy, and not sacrifice." Once again, God values the motivation and actions of a good heart over outward conformance to legalistic rules.

So then, who is making the right judgment? The Pharisees, standing on the Torah and oral tradition, declare the disciples guilty. Jesus, standing on his own authority, declares them not guilty. Is Jesus placing himself above Moses? Yes, far above. "For the Son of Man is lord of the Sabbath." Jesus claims authority over the Sabbath and the right to judge what is permissible and what is not. And he is not done yet!

Sabbath Work

The second prohibited Sabbath activity was healing. Jesus healed the man with the withered hand. Again, he does not deny that healing was work. It was the work of Jesus' ministry or "doing good." He declared that this work was lawful on the Sabbath. Jesus used the example of a sheep that had fallen into a pit. Should a man let the sheep die on the Sabbath because it would be work to lift it out? Of course not! If it was, in this case, lawful to do good to a sheep, certainly it was also lawful to do good to a man with a withered hand. This was the judgment of the "lord of the Sabbath."

But the Pharisees would accept none of Jesus' interpretations. To them, the letter of the Law was clear: if a man worked on the Sabbath, he must die. In addition to the personal penalty, the nation must be protected from an influential teacher who threatened to lead them into breaking their covenant with God.

Take a Walk

Now I will examine the second pivotal passage concerning rest. The setting is Jerusalem. Jesus heals an invalid and tells him to "take up your bed and walk." You can guess what day it was.

> Now that day was the Sabbath. So the Jews said to the man who had been healed, "It is the Sabbath, and it is not lawful for you to take up your bed." But he answered them, "The man who healed me, that man said to me, 'Take up your bed, and walk.'" They asked him, "Who is the man who said to you, Take up your bed and walk'?" Now the man who had been healed did not know who it was, for Jesus had withdrawn, as there was a crowd in the place. Afterward Jesus found him in the temple and said to him, "See, you are well! Sin no more, that nothing worse may happen to you." The man went away and told the Jews that it was Jesus who had healed him. And this was why the Jews were persecuting Jesus, because he was doing these things on the Sabbath. But Jesus answered them, "My Father is working until now, and I am working." This was why the Jews were seeking all the more to kill him, because not only was he breaking the Sabbath, but he was even calling God his own Father, making himself equal with God.
>
> John 5:9-18

Like the passage in Matthew, this is the first significant recorded conflict with the Jewish leaders in John's Gospel. It concerned Sabbath observance and resulted in the Jews seeking to kill Jesus. The specific offenses: 1) the healed man was carrying his bed, 2) Jesus had healed him and 3) told him to carry it. The Sabbath, by Law, was for rest. These activities were work.

Again, Jesus does not attempt to lawyerize his way out of the charge of working. Instead he says something astounding: "My Father is working until now, and I am working." Jesus worked on the Sabbath. And his authority claim is even more direct than calling himself "the lord of the Sabbath." Here he calls God his "Father." This is not subtle and the Jews correctly interpreted its implications. Jesus was "making himself equal with God." In other words, Jesus claimed to be God and, therefore, possessed the authority of God over Sabbath practice and everything else.

In a parallel passage, Jesus adds this: "The Sabbath was made for man, not man for the Sabbath" (Mark 2:27). With these words Jesus recalls the original intent—something that apparently had been lost in all the extrapolation of prohibited actions. Sabbath rest was to benefit the Jews.

Retreat to the Wilderness

If Jesus worked on the Sabbath, when did he rest?

> The apostles returned to Jesus and told him all that they had done and taught. And he said to them, "Come away by yourselves to a desolate place and rest a while." For many were coming and going, and they had no leisure even to eat. And they went away in the boat to a desolate place by themselves.
>
> Mark 6:30-32

The Gospels reveal that Jesus took regular breaks from his work of ministry to rest. His rest was *not* ministering, so he sought out "desolate places" away from the crowds he ministered to. We know that Jesus prayed to his Father and conversed with his disciples during these times but not much else.

Interestingly, there is no identified connection between these times of rest and Sabbath observance. In fact, in Mark 1:21-35, Jesus rises early on the morning *after* the Sabbath and goes to a desolate place to pray. This was a time of rest away from work, to refresh himself after work, in order to be able to do more work. Although the retreats in the desolate places were sometimes interrupted by the crowds that followed him, this rest appears to have been a regular practice for both Jesus and his disciples, as in this passage: "...and great crowds gathered to hear him and to be healed of their infirmities. But he would withdraw to desolate places and pray" (Lk. 5:15-16).

So...what?

To sum up, Sabbath observance was a major point of contention between Jesus and the Jewish leaders. On one hand, Jesus claimed authority over Sabbath observance and worked on the Sabbath. On the other, he rested regularly, apparently without regard to the particular day.

For Christians this raises more questions than it answers. It does not even conclusively answer the question: "When do you rest?" Nor does it address the larger issue of the relationship between the Gospel and the Law. Further research in the remainder of the New Testament is required.

CHAPTER FIVE

Rest Freedom

How should you interpret Jesus' life and words? Our Lord did not leave you to flounder. He promised to explain everything: "But the Helper, the Holy Spirit, whom the Father will send in my name, he will teach you all things and bring to your remembrance all that I have said to you" (John 14:26). Also, "When the Spirit of truth comes, he will guide you into all the truth...." (John 16:13). The Holy Spirit will teach you and guide you.

How?

> For this reason I, Paul, a prisoner for Christ Jesus on behalf of you Gentiles—assuming that you have heard of the stewardship of God's grace that was given to me for you, how the mystery was made known to me by revelation, as I have written briefly. When you read this, you can perceive my insight into the mystery of Christ, which was not made known to the sons of men in other generations as it has now been revealed to his holy apostles and prophets by the Spirit.
>
> Ephesians 3:1-5

Jesus, through his Spirit, through his Apostles, wrote the authorized commentary on himself, which explains what he meant and why he did what he did. Furthermore, Jesus, the Cornerstone of the Church, describes the Apostles as the foundation of the Church. Much of their work was to establish the basis for full understanding and practice of the Christian faith.

The Apostles did this by writing the Epistles. Much of their teaching directly explains the relationship between the Gospel and the Mosaic Law. In fact, this is the major theme that runs through Romans, Galatians and Hebrews, as well as portions of other letters.

To learn the full scope of the apostles' teaching on Gospel verses Law, you will have to study the New Testament on your own. But I will sum up very briefly: There is neither Jew nor Gentile in Christ—we are one in him. Christians are not under the Mosaic Law—we are under grace. It is not our work but Jesus' that justifies us before God. This is the New Covenant, which has replaced the Old Covenant. These are the great truths of the Christian faith. And they separate Christianity from Judaism.

To return to our subject, I will now explore the Bible's specific instruction on the Christian's practice of rest. If you had never read the Epistles, you would expect to find a great deal on this topic. After all, Sabbath rest was both a central tenet of the Mosaic Law as well as the pivotal conflict in the Gospels. So the obvious question is: What new rest commands are you to follow?

Where is the Rule Book?

Surprisingly, there isn't any! Instead, you are warned *against* subjecting yourself to the legal requirements of the Mosaic Law or to anyone else who wants to make rules for you for any other reason.

> Therefore let no one pass judgment on you in questions of food and drink, or with regard to a festival or a new moon or a Sabbath. These are a shadow of the things to come, but the substance belongs to Christ.
>
> Colossians 2:16-17

Paul says that Sabbath observance was only a shadow cast by the substance, which is Christ. More about this shortly. For now, note that nobody is to be your judge on these matters. There are no rest laws for you and don't let anyone impose any on you. Why not?

> Formerly, when you did not know God, you were enslaved to those that by nature are not gods. But now that you have come to know God, or rather to be known by God, how can you turn back again to the weak and worthless

elementary principles of the world, whose slaves you want
to be once more? You observe days and months and
seasons and years! I am afraid I may have labored over you
in vain.

Galatians 4:8-11

"Observing days"—the Sabbath and other Jewish holy days—is to
return to the "weak and worthless elementary principles of the world."
that is, law-keeping as a means of justification. This is incompatible
with the Gospel and Paul condemns it in the strongest terms: "You are
severed from Christ, you who would be justified by the law; you have
fallen away from grace" (Galations 5:4). Mosaic Law is contrasted with
Gospel or grace. This theme is pervasive throughout the Epistles.
Sabbath observance, as required by Mosaic Law, is not binding on
Christians because the entire Mosaic Law is not binding upon you. The
Old Covenant was replaced by the New Covenant. Law was replaced
by grace.

In speaking of a new covenant, he makes the first one
obsolete. And what is becoming obsolete and growing old
is ready to vanish away.

Hebrews 8:13

Some teach that portions of Mosaic Law, including the command
to rest on the Sabbath, are binding upon Christians. They are not. The
Law is now obsolete and the only biblical *requirement* to rest on the
Sabbath—or at any other particular time—was in the Mosaic Law.
Specific rest observance was not commanded before it or after it.

A parallel may be drawn with eating. Eating was also established
prior to the Law...obviously. The Law established certain eating
prohibitions that were binding on the Jews. Violating these dietary laws
broke their Covenant with God. Did eating become obsolete when the
Law passed away? No. Only the Law's restrictions on eating became
obsolete. Jesus said, "'Do you not see that whatever goes into a person
from outside cannot defile him, since it enters not his heart but his
stomach, and is expelled?' (Thus he declared all foods clean.)" (Mark
7:18-19). Like most of Jesus' sayings, this is further explained and
developed in the Acts and the Epistles.

To God Be the Glory

Do Christians, therefore, have no law or limit of any kind? Are you free to rest however you please? Yes...and no. Your freedom is constrained by your love for Jesus.

> "All things are lawful," but not all things are helpful. "All things are lawful," but not all things build up. Let no one seek his own good, but the good of his neighbor. ...So, whether you eat or drink, or whatever you do, do all to the glory of God.
>
> I Corinthians 10:23-24, 31

And again.

> And whatever you do, in word or deed, do everything in the name of the Lord Jesus, giving thanks to God the Father through him.
>
> Colossians 3:17

Your rest, like everything else, should glorify God. In Christ you are *free* to do this! Grace is not a license to selfishly indulge yourself. *This is my time and I'll do what I want! Neither is it: My work is God's time and my rest is my time. I'm off the clock.* No. All of your time is God's time. Grace compels you to selflessly honor your Lord in all things. The right perspective is: *My Master has provided this gift of rest that I may refresh myself from my work. I will thankfully accept it and honor him through it.*

When do you rest? Whenever—and however—you want to, as long as you honor the Lord.

So the New Covenant Christian enjoys freedom in his practice of rest, seeking to please Christ. He, unlike the Old Covenant Jew, is not is bound by the strictures of the Law, seeking to please Moses. This can be summed up as:

Covenant	Covenant People	Practice of Rest	Principle
New	Christians	Freedom, no regulations	Do all things to the glory of God!

What I have described is simply grace expressed in the area of rest. Because Jesus loves you, you love him. Because you love him, you seek to obey and honor him in everything—whether it is work or rest.

CHAPTER SIX

Future Rest

Time to recap. So far I have described rest through three major biblical epochs—Creation, Old Covenant and New Covenant. There is one remaining: Re-Creation.

In relation to time, Creation was in the beginning, the Old Covenant was for the Jews in the past, the New Covenant is for Christians in the present, and the Re-Creation will be at some point and beyond in the future. I contend that the work-rest order extends through all of these periods. The cycle of work followed by rest was, is and will be the experience of mankind.

Saint Peter and the Pearly Gates

Wait, wait, wait! Hold on! I'll go along with the first three, but what do you mean that there will be work in the Re-Creation? Are you talking about heaven? Work in heaven? I think not. It will be all rest.

I expected some disagreement here. I'll bet that you have said this a time or two:

I'll rest when I get to heaven!

Or the longer version:

Because my time of earth is short, I must serve the Lord
(i.e. work) without ceasing. When I die my soul will fly up
to heaven. Saint Peter will greet me at the pearly gates

30

and—after many jokes, apparently—will issue me a
glowing halo and a golden harp. I will be just like an angel,
a spirit not an embodied being. Then I will spend eternity
floating around on clouds and singing the praises of God.
This is the rest that I will receive after my arduous labor on
this miserable dust ball of a planet.

Yeah. What's wrong with it…aside from the Saint Peter jokes?
Only two things. First, it isn't entirely biblical. Second, it denigrates
the value of your present work and rest.

Two States

What occurs during the time between the death of the body and the
resurrection of the body? Theologians call this period the *intermediate
state*. Where is the soul? Is it conscious? What is happening? I am sure
you have an opinion on these matters. I do too, but I will keep it to
myself.

Then why did you bring it up?
I brought it up only to say that the intermediate state is just that—
intermediate. It is not the Christian's *final* state. While the nature of the
intermediate state is shrouded, to say the least, there are a few things
that are very clear in Scripture about the final state. One is that
Christians will have bodies. You will receive your new body at the
resurrection. You will possess this body for eternity. This is good
because embodiment is the natural condition for humanity. Since the
resurrection of the body is one of the fundamentals of the faith and
there is no disagreement on this point among those who believe the
Bible, I will dispense with any proof texts.

The second thing that is clear about the final state is that Christians
will be on the earth.

But what about all the verses that say Christians will be in heaven, like these:

For we know that if the tent that is our earthly home is
destroyed, we have a building from God, a house not
made with hands, eternal in the heavens. For in this tent
we groan, longing to put on our heavenly dwelling, if
indeed by putting it on we may not be found naked.

II Corinthians 5:1-3

> But our citizenship is in heaven, and from it we await a
> Savior, the Lord Jesus Christ, who will transform our lowly
> body to be like his glorious body, by the power that
> enables him even to subject all things to himself.
>
> Philippians 3:20-21

> According to his great mercy, he has caused us to be born
> again to a living hope through the resurrection of Jesus
> Christ from the dead, to an inheritance that is
> imperishable, undefiled, and unfading, kept in heaven for
> you....
>
> I Peter 1:3-4

Actually, these verses do not say that heaven is the residence of a Christian for eternity. Your dwelling is in heaven. Your citizenship is in heaven. Your inheritance is in heaven. Yes, all of these are in heaven *now*. Peter says, a little more fully, that these things are "kept in heaven." They are kept in heaven now because Jesus is in heaven now. But because he is there now does not mean he will stay there.

Where He Goes I Will Follow

One thing is certain, though. Wherever the Shepherd leads, his sheep will follow. Wherever the King reigns, his subjects will serve him. Wherever the Bridegroom is, his bride will be also. The passages below make this clear:

> And if I go and prepare a place for you, I will come again
> and will take you to myself, that where I am you may be
> also.
>
> John 14:3

> If then you have been raised with Christ, seek the things
> that are above, where Christ is, seated at the right hand of
> God. Set your minds on things that are above, not on
> things that are on earth. For you have died, and your life is
> hidden with Christ in God. When Christ who is your life
> appears, then you also will appear with him in glory.
>
> Colossians 3:1-4

So where is Jesus and where does he go? At his ascension from earth to heaven two angels explained this to the apostles.

> And while they were gazing into heaven as he went,
> behold, two men stood by them in white robes, and said,
> "Men of Galilee, why do you stand looking into heaven?
> This Jesus, who was taken up from you into heaven, will
> come in the same way as you saw him go into heaven."
>
> Acts 1:10-11

Total Makeover

At his appearing Jesus will "save those who are eagerly waiting for him" (Hebrews 9:28). He promises faithful elders that, "when the chief Shepherd appears, you will receive the unfading crown of glory" (I Peter 5:4). And "we know that when he appears we shall be like him, because we shall see him as he is" (I John 3:2). All of these things—salvation, reward and transformation—happen at Jesus' return. Paul calls this the "blessed hope, the appearing of the glory of our great God and Savior Jesus Christ" (Titus 2:13).

The "blessed hope" is not that your soul flies up to heaven after you die. It is that Jesus will return to earth and resurrect you. When he does, the Apostle Peter describes the scene.

> But the day of the Lord will come like a thief, and then the
> heavens will pass away with a roar, and the heavenly
> bodies will be burned up and dissolved, and the earth and
> the works that are done on it will be exposed. Since all
> these things are thus to be dissolved, what sort of people
> ought you to be in lives of holiness and godliness, waiting
> for and hastening the coming of the day of God, because
> of which the heavens will be set on fire and dissolved, and
> the heavenly bodies will melt as they burn! But according
> to his promise we are waiting for new heavens and a new
> earth in which righteousness dwells.
>
> II Peter 3:10-13

At the final judgment the existing universe will be destroyed and replaced by the new heavens and earth or, as some think, the old will be purified through fire to produce the new. Either way, there will be a new heaven and earth. What happens to the universe as a whole also happens to Christians individually. Your corrupted body will be redeemed and replaced by a much better model.

> For the creation waits with eager longing for the revealing of the sons of God. For the creation was subjected to futility, not willingly, but because of him who subjected it, in hope that the creation itself will be set free from its bondage to corruption and obtain the freedom of the glory of the children of God. For we know that the whole creation has been groaning together in the pains of childbirth until now. And not only the creation, but we ourselves, who have the firstfruits of the Spirit, groan inwardly as we wait eagerly for adoption as sons, the redemption of our bodies. For in this hope we were saved.
>
> Romans 8:19-24

And where do God and his people end up? The Apostle John tells us.

> Then I saw a new heaven and a new earth, for the first heaven and the first earth had passed away, and the sea was no more. And I saw the holy city, new Jerusalem, coming down out of heaven from God, prepared as a bride adorned for her husband. And I heard a loud voice from the throne saying, "Behold, the dwelling place of God is with man. He will dwell with them, and they will be his people, and God himself will be with them as their God.
>
> Revelation 21:1-3

I started this theology of rest in the second chapter of the first book of the Bible and have now reached the second to the last chapter of the last book. The last sentence in this passage states three times that God will be *with* man. Where? On the earth. God was with man on the old earth in a garden before the Fall, and he will again be with man on the new earth in a city after the resurrection.

This should be no surprise. Jesus promised it.

> Blessed are the meek, for they shall inherit the earth.
>
> Matthew 5:5

A New Job

And what do you think that you will be doing in a new body on the new earth that you will inherit?

It seems to me that you have wandered completely off the subject. This is interesting, but what does it have to do with rest?

You will see soon enough, friend. If there is to be rest, then there must be work. Work always precedes rest. Before you can understand future rest, you must understand future work. Admittedly the biblical teaching on this subject is not as extensive as in some other areas. However, there is enough scriptural light to interpret by.

I will return to the Gospels because it is in Jesus' kingdom teaching that we first see future work.

> For it [the kingdom of heaven] will be like a man going on a journey, who called his servants and entrusted to them his property. To one he gave five talents, to another two, to another one, to each according to his ability. Then he went away. He who had received the five talents went at once and traded with them, and he made five talents more. So also he who had the two talents made two talents more. But he who had received the one talent went and dug in the ground and hid his master's money. Now after a long time the master of those servants came and settled accounts with them.
> Matthew 25:14-19

You are familiar with this parable. The servant who buries the master's money is condemned. But note what the master says to those servants who obtain a good return on his investment.

> Well done, good and faithful servant. You have been faithful over a little; I will set you over much. Enter into the joy of your master.... For to everyone who has will more be given, and he will have an abundance.
> Matthew 25:21-29

This parable has most often been interpreted to mean that you should use what you possess to serve God, which is why common usage of the word talent has become *gift, ability or skill*. The interpretation is correct, as far as it goes, and you usually apply it by

35

pressuring your children to play the piano during the offertory at church. But this does not go far enough.

Jesus is clearly referring to his return and judgment. Stewardship is very serious business and has eternal consequences. Note that the master says to each of the good stewards: "You have been faithful over a little; I will set you over much." In a parallel passage (Luke 19) each servant receives a mina, about three months' wages. The servant who turns his mina into ten "shall have authority over ten cities." The servant who turns his mina into five shall "be over five cities."

What does this mean? The interpretation is that steward—servants who have faithfully fulfilled their responsibilities will receive greater responsibilities in the kingdom to come at Jesus' appearing. To put it bluntly, as every boss likes to say: "The reward for good work is more work." Remember that God created man for work in the first place. Only at the Fall did work become toilsome. In the beginning work was without thorns and it shall be again.

Perhaps you are not yet convinced. Perhaps you think that I make too much of the small details in these parables. While this is an interpretive danger, the future reward for faithful stewardship is not a small detail. It is one of the significant points. You may also think that a future reward is spoken of here but not work. To which I would reply that you are evading the plain meaning of the text. The future reward is *more work*. Or if you think that managing or ruling is not work, then you have done neither.

Still, to base this all on parables is precarious. That is so. Fortunately, there are a few additional glimpses in the Scripture.

> You are those who have stayed with me in my trials, and I assign to you, as my Father assigned to me, a kingdom, that you may eat and drink at my table in my kingdom and sit on thrones judging the twelve tribes of Israel.
>
> Luke 22:28-30

Jesus promises his disciples a kingdom. In this kingdom they will eat, drink and judge (i.e. rule). Future food and work. This is the parable of the talents applied to the disciples. This is plain teaching not wrapped in story. Jesus has repeated the same truth in several different ways. Present work determines future work. The reward for good work is more work. Faithfulness with little leads to being entrusted with more.

Everlasting Work

The final description of the Christian's eternal vocation is given to the John the Apostle. The Book of Revelation concludes with a vision of the new heaven and earth, the New Jerusalem descending to the new earth, and a description of the New Jerusalem. This description ends with these words:

> And I saw no temple in the city, for its temple is the Lord God the Almighty and the Lamb. And the city has no need of sun or moon to shine on it, for the glory of God gives it light, and its lamp is the Lamb. By its light will the nations walk, and the kings of the earth will bring their glory into it, and its gates will never be shut by day—and there will be no night there. They will bring into it the glory and the honor of the nations. …No longer will there be anything accursed, but the throne of God and of the Lamb will be in it, and his servants will worship him. They will see his face, and his name will be on their foreheads. And night will be no more. They will need no light of lamp or sun, for the Lord God will be their light, and they will reign forever and ever.
>
> Revelation 21:22-22:5

While we rightfully focus our attention on God in this passage, do not miss the description of men. People are called "kings of the earth" and servants, who "will reign forever and ever." The book of Revelation is written in highly symbolic language, of course, but the symbolism means something. We must not shape this symbolism into anything we want, especially when its interpretation has been well established. *Kings of the earth* do not symbolize disembodied spirits in heaven. *Servants* do not symbolize a spirit choir singing the *Hallelujah Chorus* amongst the clouds. *Reigning* does not symbolize celestial ease. No. The description of man's role and responsibility at the very end of the Bible is consistent with God's plan and purpose for man that we have traced throughout the Bible.

Moreover, this final peek ahead is strikingly parallel to the Genesis account. God forms the earth and commissions man to rule over it. Man works and eats. But man's position definitely improves at the conclusion of Revelation. On the first earth man served as a gardener. On the new earth men will reign as kings. There is much to ponder here, but the most significant point regarding our study is that ruling and reigning, by definition, involve work.

And if there is work in the next life, there must also be rest. One must follow the other. This is the created order.

From Here to Eternity

So what difference does it make? A lot of difference, actually. If you consider the present pattern of work and rest to be a temporary experience, an anomaly, a burden to bear for a brief flash before eternity, then you will soon despise both your work and rest. *It's all going to burn anyway.* Also, it makes a difference in how you envision the future life. You can relate to something that is the same but better more than to something that is completely unimaginable. Will the redeemed rejoice in worshiping and glorifying God forever? Yes, of course. But every indication is that this will involve the full range of human work-rest experience, just as it always has.

CHAPTER SEVEN

Take a Deep Breath

In this brief theology I have assembled the major themes of the Bible. You have traveled from God to man, from innocence to falleness, from Genesis to Revelation, from Old Covenant to New Covenant, from Moses to Jesus, from this life to the next, from creation to re-creation, and from the old earth to the new earth. Throughout the journey you have seen work and rest all along the way.

You have learned that rest is always related to work, although it is always separate from it. Rest is not-work. Rest follows work. Rest refreshes from work. To put it all together, *rest is the activities that refresh you after your work.*

Regarding the questions of *when* and *how,* we have seen that rest practice was tightly defined for Jews under the Old Covenant, but that it is an area of freedom for Christians under the New Covenant. Following a basic principle of Christian living, this freedom is not to justify sinful indulgence but is an opportunity to glorify God while enjoying his gracious provision.

This should be simple and clear, but it may not be enough for you. Perhaps you are not yet convinced. Instead of finding joy in rest and giving thanks to God for it, you may still have deep uncertainty about rest, viewing it only as a necessary concession to your human weaknesses or even as outright sin.

This flows, I think, from another area of your theology. Confusion about rest is just a subset of a larger misunderstanding about living in the present world. This I will begin to explore in the next chapter.

CHAPTER EIGHT

Two Buckets

Are you comfortable with rest yet? Are you ready to buy a cabin? Or is something bothering you?

Well…there is something. I can't quite put my finger on it.

Let me help. You still have a nagging, troubling, deep sense of unease with rest, even guilt. How can I explain it?

Ah…imagine that you carry two buckets through life. Now visualize all of your activities as tennis balls. One tennis ball materializes for each thing that you do. As you walk through life you drop each ball into one or the other of these buckets

Your problem with rest is caused by the labels that you place on your buckets. I will describe your labels in a moment. But first let me describe the labels I think you should use. These labels use biblical terminology and reflect biblical concepts. At this point you should know what they are.

One is a work bucket and the other is a rest bucket. (There is actually a third bucket—idleness—but I will keep things simple for now.) Every tennis ball—every activity—goes either into the work bucket or into the

rest bucket. The balls in the work bucket fulfill your vocational calling and the balls in the rest bucket refresh you from your work. When the two buckets are filled properly they provide a good balance between work and rest.

Now it is time to fill the buckets. Below is a list of sample activities and the bucket I have placed them into.

Activity	Bucket
Make Widgets on the Job	Work
Make Widgets for a Hobby	Rest
Play Board Games	Rest
Wash Laundry	Work
Watch Football	Rest
Play Football Professionally	Work
Play Football with Friends	Rest
Teach Sunday School	Work
Attend Sunday School	Rest
Read a Novel	Rest
Witness to Neighbor	Work
Bowl on Team	Rest
Read the Bible and Pray	Rest
Spend time at the cabin	Rest

I know that you may want to debate some of this bucketing, but let us not quibble like the Pharisees. The main point here is only that you can categorize what you do into either work or rest activities. In this, the Pharisees were correct. Remember that they were concerned with obedience to the Mosaic Law, the Old Covenant. Work during the time for rest was a serious violation of the Law—covenant breaking! So it was very important for Jews to know which balls went into which buckets.

You, the Christian, will not become a covenant breaker by mixing up the buckets. You just need to be able to distinguish between your work and rest so that you can do both well. You do not seek legalistic righteousness in your rest but only to become refreshed from your work.

Your Labels

If you label your buckets as work and rest, you should have a healthy and balanced view of rest. In fact, your theology of rest is sufficient and I can improve it no more. Move on to the next section of the book. There is no need to swallow the medicine if you are not sick.

Still with me? Different labels? I thought so. Your labels reveal some theological knots that will be difficult to untangle. What are the labels on your two buckets? Instead of *work* and *rest*, you may have:

Secular and *Sacred*
Unspiritual and *Spiritual*

Or perhaps the particularly Evangelical emphasis:

Not Sharing the Gospel and *Sharing the Gospel*

While the terminology is different, each of these categorizations spring from the same theological root. But before I identify this, notice that the first label in each set has a negative connotation and the second label has a positive connotation. The stuff in the first bucket is bad and the stuff in the second bucket is good. This is not the case if you have work and rest buckets. There is no negative connotation to "work." Some *particular types* of work may be inherently bad, such as thievery, but the category of work itself is neither bad nor good. The same is true for rest. Binge drinking, for example, is a bad rest activity, while prayer is a good one.

Perhaps "bad" is too strong a word for everything that you place in the first bucket. Bad is just another word for sinful. If you only have these two buckets to put activities into, then whatever does not belong in your Sacred/Spiritual/Gospel bucket belongs in the other bucket. Lots of activities are going to go into this bucket, but you would not say that all of them are outright sinful. Some of the activities may be necessary because of your physical existence and temporal needs. You would not say that sleeping or taking a shower is sinful, of course, but you would not label these as sacred activities either, so they belong in the first bucket. But whether they are outright sinful or just of earthly necessity, you consider the activities that you place into this bucket to be ultimately worthless in contrast with Sacred/Spiritual/Gospel activities, which you consider to be eternally valuable. So I will say that your labels are:

TWO BUCKETS

Ultimately Worthless   **Eternally Valuable**

Now I will revisit the same list of activities as before and categorize according to your buckets.

Activity	Bucket
Make Widgets on the Job	Ultimately Worthless
Make Widgets for a Hobby	Ultimately Worthless
Play Board Games	Ultimately Worthless
Wash Laundry	Ultimately Worthless
Watch Football	Ultimately Worthless
Play Football Professionally	Ultimately Worthless
Play Football with Friends	Ultimately Worthless
Teach Sunday School	Eternally Valuable
Attend Sunday School	Eternally Valuable
Read a Novel	Ultimately Worthless
Witness to Neighbor	Eternally Valuable
Bowl on Team	Ultimately Worthless
Read the Bible and Pray	Eternally Valuable
Spend time at the cabin	Ultimately Worthless

Look again at the first list and compare it to the second list. Did you notice that all the activities categorized as rest in the first list are labeled as "worthless" in the second, except Sunday School, Bible reading and prayer? That is why you feel guilty over the rest activities that you label as "secular", "unspiritual" or not evangelistic. You think that they have no or little value. Your theology informs you that these things are wasting your time and life.

The problem is that you often rest in these ways. You rest in these ways because you require these particular rest activities in order to be refreshed from your work, just as you breathe because you require air or eat because you require food.

But…can't I "redeem" those worthless rest activities by combining them with

43

something that has ultimate worth? For instance, if I witness to my teammates when bowling, won't that make it an eternally valuable activity? Or if I prepare for Bible study while I'm at the cabin, won't it become time profitably spent.

You are assuming that rest for rest's sake is not sufficient to justify the activity. You feel the need to legitimize your rest by mixing in some "spiritual" work. You are simply proving the point that you categorize activities along these lines, instead of a work-rest division.

Uh-huh.

Re-Sizing the Buckets

I can see that you are committed to your labels. Consider how these shape your perspective. For instance, tell me how you view the path to Christian maturity.

That's easy. I try to limit the number of tennis balls I place in the first bucket and place as many balls as possible in the second bucket.

So you try to make one bucket as small as possible and the other as large as possible, like this?

Ultimately   Eternally
Worthless   Valuable

Of course…isn't that what I am supposed to be doing?

Everything/Whatever Christianity

If your labels are right, your logic is sound. But if your labels are wrong you will find yourself frustrated and confused, as is the poor fellow who keeps trying to pound a round peg into a square hole. But there is a better way. As I noted earlier, the New Testament consistently presents a much different perspective.

For **everything** created by God is good, and nothing is to be rejected if it is received with thanksgiving, for it is made holy by the word of God and prayer.

I Timothy 4:4-5

So, whether you eat or drink, or **whatever you do**, do all to the glory of God.

I Corinthians 10:31

And **whatever you do**, in word or deed, do everything in the name of the Lord Jesus, giving thanks to God the Father through him.

Colossians 3:17

One of the most striking features about Christianity is that you are required to honor Jesus in *everything*, in *whatever*, not just in "religious" activities. But your buckets categorize and value every activity by whether or not you consider it to be religious. Your worldview makes a division that Jesus and the Apostles erased.

Each of your activities will be judged not by its label but by its virtue. The "why" matters more than the "what." You can sin against God while at church and you can glorify him while plowing the cornfield. The question is, are you aiming at his glory or not?

Therefore, every one of your activities has eternal consequences. Your faithfulness or faithlessness will be reviewed by Jesus at the great judgment. This is why Christians are commanded to bring all aspects of life—all of work and all of rest—into submission to Jesus. He will judge all, everything, whatever. And since he will, each of your activities is important and has great value.

But I can tell that you are hesitant to peel off your old "valuable" and "worthless" labels and replace them with "work" and "rest." The old labels have been on your buckets so long that you are going to have to scrape them off with your fingernails bit by bit. I'll try to help.

CHAPTER NINE

Secular Work

Let's take a closer look at your "secular" bucket.

Do I have to? This is making me uncomfortable. I'm used to things the way they are.

I'm afraid so. It is the only way that you will be able to correct your labels.

You have not convinced me to do that yet…but go ahead and make your case. I'll listen a bit longer.

That's sporting. So consider your job—your means of earning your bread. If you classify your job as "secular," then you are really saying that it is ultimately worthless from an eternal perspective. So, if this is your opinion, what is the reasonable thing to do? The obvious answer is to trade your secular job in for a sacred one. Quit that job making widgets in the factory and become a missionary, for example. Widget making, after all, ranks at the bottom of your spirituality scale and missionary service ranks at the top. Widget-making is "worldly" while serving as a missionary builds the kingdom. Widget-making is third class and missionary work is first class. Widget-making does not earn many God points while being a missionary hits the jackpot. It follows that every dedicated, sincere Christian should pursue sacred vocational work, if not full-time at least in some short-term or part-time venues. Improve your position.

Hey – that's what I'm thinking! I despise my factory job. I want my life to count for something!

Everything counts, my friend, even widget making. At least Jesus seemed to think so.

SECULAR WORK

Tax Collectors

If there is a job that can be categorized as worthless, it is certainly that of tax collector. The tax collector was a despised vocation in Jesus day, just as it is in ours. People who pay taxes do not highly value the labor of those who collect them. But a tax collector in first century Judea was even more repugnant, as he was the willing servant of the oppressive Roman occupation. We have recorded conversations between Jesus and two tax collectors.

One was named Zacchaeus (Luke 19:1-10). When Jesus was passing by, Zacchaeus wanted to see him. Being a short fellow, he climbed up a tree to obtain a view over the crowds, as in the children's song:

Zacchaeus was a wee little man, a wee little man was he
He climbed up in a Sycamore tree, for the Lord he wanted to see...

This gives the impression of a cute or comic character, but it is doubtful that his contemporaries would have considered him in this way. Zacchaeus was a chief tax collector and was rich. The general assessment was simply that he was a "sinner." Jesus, as was his custom, shocked the Jews' sensibilities and invited himself to Zacchaeus' house. Zacchaeus responded to Jesus in faith, as demonstrated by his words: "Behold, Lord, the half of my goods I give to the poor. And if I have defrauded anyone of anything, I restore it fourfold." Good works always flow from true faith. Those who love Jesus obey him.

One striking thing here is that Jesus did not direct Zacchaeus to get another job. Zacchaeus understood that being a follower of Jesus required him to make amends for the past injustices he committed at work but not to change vocations.

You may object that this is an argument from silence. We do not know whether Zacchaeus resigned his position in the civil service or not. Fair enough. We should not base our theology on what is unclear but on what is clear. So here is what is clear—throughout the New Testament the extensive and consistent teaching is that we serve and honor God in *whatever* vocation we find ourselves. This theme began with the teaching of John the Baptist as he prepared the way for Jesus:

Tax collectors also came to be baptized and said to him,
"Teacher, what shall we do?" And he said to them,
"Collect no more than you are authorized to do." Soldiers

47

also asked him, "And we, what shall we do?" And he said to them, "Do not extort money from anyone by threats or by false accusation, and be content with your wages."
Luke 3:12-14

Tax collectors were not commanded to quit. Soldiers were not encouraged to become conscientious objectors or peace activists. In fact, the Epistles command believers to serve Christ in every possible vocation, whether master, slave, rich, poor, single, husband, wife or child. Following Jesus does not require a change of vocations. There are exceptions, of course, which bring us to the second tax collector.

A Second Calling

Matthew (or Levi) is well known to us from the Gospels. Like Zacchaeus, his notorious profession is undoubtedly the reason he receives special mention. Jesus told Matthew to "follow me." This general command did not require a vocational change for Matthew. Jesus called upon *everyone* to follow him, as here:

And calling the crowd to him with his disciples, he said to them, "If anyone would come after me, let him deny himself and take up his cross and follow me.
Mark 8:34

However, Matthew received a second calling from Jesus. This one required a vocational change.

And he went up on the mountain and called to him those whom he desired, and they came to him. And he appointed twelve (whom he also named apostles) so that they might be with him and he might send them out to preach and have authority to cast out demons. He appointed the twelve....
Mark 3:13-16

The apostles received a new vocation with this calling. They were to be with Jesus as he ministered, and he would send them out on ministry trips of their own. Matthew would no longer be a tax collector or Peter a fisherman. Not everyone who followed Jesus was called to be an apostle or to other full-time work. Only twelve received this call

48

out of thousands. The apostles were the exception not the rule.

This is also the clear teaching in the Epistles. Every Christian is called to follow Jesus, to serve him in and through vocation, *whatever* it may be. A few are called to full-time ministry work. The qualification for a full-time ministry position is not sincerity, enthusiasm, commitment, zeal or dedication. The qualification for full-time ministry is giftedness. For example: "Let the elders who rule well be considered worthy of double honor, especially those who labor in preaching and teaching" (I Timothy 5:17). All elders are worthy of honor because of their service to Christ. Some elders, those with evident gifting in preaching and teaching, are to receive "double honor," that is, the addition of pay. All elders do the work of ministry. Some get paid so that they may do more of it.

To sum up, work is work—whether or not you are paid for it and regardless of whether or not it accomplishes some type of formal ministry. The factory worker can glorify God through his widget making just as much as the teaching elder can through his preaching. Each has his own vocational calling. This is not a new and revelatory insight. Do you remember the Protestant Reformation?

Forgotten History

Prior to the Reformation the secular-sacred dichotomy had become institutionalized throughout the Church, especially in the area of vocation. "Sacred" versus "secular" labels were on everyone's buckets. For the Roman Catholic Church, the monks, nuns, priests and hermits thought their labors were all going into an eternally valuable bucket while everyone else had to settle for depositing their work into an ultimately worthless bucket.

One of Martin Luther's major contributions was to return to a biblical perspective, which he described as the "priesthood of all believers." Luther erased the sacred-secular distinction and returned the full scope of human experience and endeavors to the arena of godly living. Sadly, we seem to have forgotten this truth. We assume that it is pastors, missionaries, Christian school teachers, seminary professors, para-church workers, etc., who are filling their buckets full of eternal rewards while the rest of us laggards do not have much to show for our worldly efforts. These misleading vocational classifications still falsely distinguish those who are really serious about serving God from those who are not. This should not be.

Now what about rest? Admittedly there is less direct scriptural material in the New Testament addressing rest. However, if all things are created for the glory of God, what is true for the work must be true for rest. You are not commanded to reflect the image of God, express your faith, and honor Jesus in your work only to set these things aside when you rest. *I've been glorifying God in my work but now it's time to take a break from that.* No! The everything/whatever principle applies to both work and rest.

Bucket Check

It is time to carry your imaginary buckets to the final judgment. Here is the Lord Jesus, not Saint Peter, and you will stand before him in body and soul, not in unclothed soul. I do not really believe that this will be a time for joking, but humor is often helpful to bring home a point. In that spirit....

So everyone is standing in line for the judgment. Let us listen to the conversation as one Mr. Spiritual steps forward. (Note to reader: Mr. Spiritual labels his buckets the same as you do.)

> **Lord:** What is in those two buckets you carry?
> **Spiritual:** These are all of my earthly deeds.
> **Lord:** Read the labels on the buckets.
> **Spiritual:** This little tiny bucket here is labeled "Ultimately Worthless." This very, very large bucket is labeled "Eternally Valuable."
> **Lord:** Describe the contents of each bucket.
> **Spiritual:** Everything in the little bucket is the time I wasted, like my job at the widget factory. It is stubble that will now burn. But everything in the very, very large bucket is my multitudinous kingdom activities. This mountain of gold is delivered by your humble servant.
> **Lord:** Where did you come up with that theology? Never mind—it was a rhetorical question. But tell me this, why didn't you buy that cabin I provided for your refreshment?
> **Spiritual:** Surely not, Lord! I thought it was from the devil, so I resisted the temptation. More gold for me... er... I mean for you.
> **Lord:** I see.
> **Spiritual:** How I labored unceasingly and tirelessly to

50

build your kingdom! I have run my course. My work is done. I am looking forward to the eternal rest of heaven.
Lord: You have much to learn. Stand aside and remain silent.
Spiritual: Yes, Lord.

The next in line is one Mr. Faithful. He steps forward.

Lord: What is in those two buckets you carry?
Faithful: These are all of my earthly deeds.
Lord: Read the labels on the buckets.
Faithful: This bucket is labeled "Work" and the other "Rest."
Lord: Just as I intended. They are well balanced too.
Faithful: Thank you, my Lord.
Lord: How shall I judge you?
Faithful: The contents in each bucket that dishonored you are stubble that will now be burned. The contents that honored you are the gold.
Lord: Correct again! But I have one thing against you.
Faithful: Lord?
Lord: Do you see that knucklehead standing over there?
Faithful: Yes, Lord.
Lord: Why didn't you help him improve his theology? I gifted him with the ability to make widgets for my glory. Instead, he became a preacher, which is not his strength…to say the least. He messed things up even more by working himself to death, refusing to take proper rest. Worst of all, he didn't buy that cabin.
Faithful: Forgive me, Lord.
Lord: Of course. But on the New Earth you will instruct him in a better way…after his shift is completed at the new widget factory.
Faithful: Yes, Lord.

You see, I am attempting to make things a little smoother for you at the last judgment. But I know that you are not quite ready to change the labels on your buckets. What you need is the proper perspective about life in the here-and-now and its relationship to the spiritual realm.

CHAPTER TEN

Spiritual Rest

What is still keeping you from putting work and rest labels on your buckets? I think it is the way you define and understand these five concepts: spiritual, holiness, world, earth and flesh. Together these describe your understanding of living—working and resting—in the material universe. If your understanding is wrong, your labels will be wrong, which they are. This is the root of your mislabeling. And it is time to dig it out.

No Matter

I will begin with *spiritual*. What is the biblical definition? This is a difficult question. The use of the term is extensive and nuanced throughout the Epistles but not elsewhere in the Bible. In general it refers to what is unseen.

> For we do not wrestle against flesh and blood, but against the rulers, against the authorities, against the cosmic powers over this present darkness, against the spiritual forces of evil in the heavenly places."
> Ephesians 6:12

In this verse the curtain is drawn back and we get a glimpse of the spiritual realm. Note that good and evil, angels and demons, reside in the "heavenly places" and that there is interaction between this place and our own realm, the physical realm. In addition to this unseen warfare, the spiritual realm contains unseen blessings, the multifaceted riches of salvation in Jesus.

> Blessed be the God and Father of our Lord Jesus Christ,
> who has blessed us in Christ with every spiritual blessing in
> the heavenly places...."
>
> Ephesians 1:3

Reality consists of both realms—the physical and the spiritual. The one we comprehend by sight; the other by faith. There are some exceptions recorded in the Bible when the spiritual realm is seen – the appearance of angels, for instance – but these are clearly unusual events and not the norm. We do not usually see angels. They are real but unseen, as are spiritual blessings, heaven, etc.

In biblical usage a "spiritual" man is not a non-physical person or one who has mystically transcended this world in order to abide in the spiritual realm. No. He is one who lives his physical life in the light of spiritual reality, believing what God has revealed in the Scripture. Spiritual words speak of these truths. Spiritual songs sing of them.

Although Jesus does not use the word "spiritual," his teaching is the foundation for what is amplified in the Epistles. I will examine one passage on this subject from the Gospels. But first consider Jesus' teaching style. It was...unusual, to say the least. He continuously astounded and challenged those who heard him. The responses of his listeners were not usually recorded, but I imagine they were most often along this line: *What is the connection? Why did he refer to that? Where is he going with this?* I can imagine these reactions because they are my reactions. Jesus, the Master Teacher, uses the technique of teaching spiritual truths through comparison and contrast with physical things. He talks about being "born again" with Nicodemus and about "living water" with the woman at the well, to give a few examples. His parables display the same method but in story form. This is the technique Jesus uses when he refers to food to explain a spiritual truth.

Spiritual Food

> Do not labor for the food that perishes, but for the food
> that endures to eternal life, which the Son of Man will give
> to you. ...Jesus then said to them, "Truly, truly, I say to
> you, it was not Moses who gave you the bread from
> heaven, but my Father gives you the true bread from

53

heaven. For the bread of God is he who comes down
from heaven and gives life to the world." They said to him,
"Sir, give us this bread always." Jesus said to them, "I am
the bread of life; whoever comes to me shall not hunger,
and whoever believes in me shall never thirst. ...Whoever
feeds on my flesh and drinks my blood has eternal life, and
I will raise him up on the last day. For my flesh is true
food, and my blood is true drink. Whoever feeds on my
flesh and drinks my blood abides in me, and I in him.
...When many of his disciples heard it, they said, "This is a
hard saying; who can listen to it?" But Jesus, knowing in
himself that his disciples were grumbling about this, said to
them, "Do you take offense at this? Then what if you were
to see the Son of Man ascending to where he was before?
It is the Spirit who gives life; the flesh is no help at all. The
words that I have spoken to you are spirit and life.
John 6:27-63

Here is the connection between working and eating once again. You
work in order to eat. Jesus takes this progression one step further. You
eat in order to live. Here is the entire sequence: You work in order to
eat in order to live. Physical food nourishes you temporarily. You eat
it and are able to live physically for a while in this world. But physical
food perishes and so eventually will your body that is sustained by it.

Jesus says that there is another kind of work, another kind of food,
and another kind of life. This other kind, in contrast to the physical, is
spiritual. Faith is the spiritual work. You must believe in Jesus. Jesus is
the spiritual food, the true bread, the bread of God, the bread of life,
the true food. This food nourishes you for eternity, that is, Jesus gives
you eternal life. He is eternal life. You must have faith in Jesus in order
to eat Jesus and have eternal life. Spiritual work (belief), food (Jesus)
and life (eternal life) corresponds to physical work, food and life.

So there is a parallel between the spiritual and physical but there is
also a contrast. Here is the first line again: "Do not labor for the food
that perishes, but for the food that endures to eternal life." Jesus is
certainly contrasting the two kinds of food, but the crucial question is
whether the contrast means that you must make a *selection* or that you
must make a *distinction*.

If the interpretation is that you must make a selection, then you
must choose only *one*. You can work either for physical food or for
spiritual food. In this understanding, Jesus must be commanding you

54

to stop working for physical food and only work for spiritual food. That is, you are to quit your job and focus solely on your faith. The physical is to be replaced by the spiritual. This may sound very devout and pietistic, but it presents a practical problem. Starvation. Inconveniences such as this do not prove that this theology is wrong, but it would limit the practitioners. More importantly, there is no such thing taught or practiced anywhere in the Bible.

The other interpretive choice is that Jesus is making a distinction between physical food and spiritual food. In this understanding, the spiritual is explained by contrast with the physical. The spiritual is in a separate class from the physical. They are different things. This seems to be the sense of the full context, as stated at the end of the passage: "It is the Spirit who gives life; the flesh is no help at all. The words that I have spoken to you are spirit and life." If I may roughly paraphrase: "You cannot eat your way to eternal life with physical food. You must partake of spiritual food that comes from the Spirit of God as explained in spiritual words."

This does not mean that physical food is contrary or opposed to eternal life. It means that it is irrelevant to eternal life. You must spiritually consume Jesus to be saved, not a particular physical diet. You must eat the Gospel not some magical beans. Nor will certain kinds of food damn you for eternity. They will simply pass through your body and perish. This is Jesus' vivid way of explaining things.

What then is the value of physical food? That is a silly question, especially if you are hungry. You require food to live. Moreover, you should enjoy food. It is a great blessing. This has always been so since Adam. Furthermore, there is a spiritual connection. Physical food should always remind you of spiritual food, that is, of Jesus. You formally make this connection when taking communion, but you should also make it when chewing every mouthful of food.

Finally, consider this. Nothing in the physical realm changed when Jesus proclaimed himself the Bread of Life. Jesus, who is spiritual food, continued to eat physical food. That is quite profound when you think about it. But there is more. He continued to eat physical food even after his resurrection.

> "Have you anything here to eat?" They gave him a piece of broiled fish, and he took it and ate before them.
> Luke 24:41b-43

Jesus saw no conflict between the physical and the spiritual regarding food. Neither should you.

Okay! You have belabored this point enough! Of course I know that I need both physical and spiritual food! What does this have to do with rest?

Just this. It is the same with rest. You need both. Spiritual rest does not eliminate physical rest. This seems obvious about food but not so obvious about rest. But I am getting ahead of myself. Walk with me a little further.

Spiritual Marriage

What about marriage? Is there a spiritual aspect of marriage concerning Jesus? If so, how does it relate to the physical aspect, that is, earthly marriage? Must you choose only one? Let us see.

> Wives, submit to your own husbands, as to the Lord. For the husband is the head of the wife even as Christ is the head of the church, his body, and is himself its Savior. Now as the church submits to Christ, so also wives should submit in everything to their husbands. Husbands, love your wives, as Christ loved the church and gave himself up for her, that he might sanctify her, having cleansed her by the washing of water with the word, so that he might present the church to himself in splendor, without spot or wrinkle or any such thing, that she might be holy and without blemish. In the same way husbands should love their wives as their own bodies. He who loves his wife loves himself. For no one ever hated his own flesh, but nourishes and cherishes it, just as Christ does the church, because we are members of his body. "Therefore a man shall leave his father and mother and hold fast to his wife, and the two shall become one flesh." This mystery is profound, and I am saying that it refers to Christ and the church.
>
> Ephesians 5:22-32

Unlike the passage on eating where the physical helps you understand the spiritual, here the spiritual (the marriage of Jesus and the Church) instructs you about the physical (your marriage). Again you see that the spiritual fulfillment of marriage in Jesus does not in any way devalue earthly marriage. Rather, it exalts its significance. A husband is to love his wife in the same way that Jesus loves his Church. The physical is to reflect the truth of the spiritual. The spiritual, the union of Jesus and his Church, does not abolish earthly marriage. You do not have to choose one or the other. In fact, physical marriage is the norm for Christians. There are exceptions, which Paul explains elsewhere, but these exceptions prove the rule. Physical marriage is not antithetical to spiritual marriage. The physical is not opposed to the spiritual. Rather, the spiritual enlightens and ennobles earthly marriage just as it does for food.

Spiritual Rest

Having explored the relationship of the spiritual to the physical, I come at last to rest itself. Is there spiritual rest? Definitely.

The greatest exposition about rest in the Bible is in the book of Hebrews, chapters three and four. This is a significant passage.

To begin, let me summarize the context and flow of the argumentation. The book of Hebrews reveals how Jesus is superior to every aspect of the Old Covenant, including Moses, the Aaronic priesthood, the tabernacle, and the sacrifices. The writer explains that these things are only a "shadow," just as Paul in Colossians said that the Sabbath was a "shadow of the things to come," and Jesus described the manna in the wilderness as a foreshadowing of himself as spiritual food. Jesus standing in the New Testament casts his shadow backward into the Old Testament. The shadow always leads to him.

> For since the law has but a shadow of the good things to come instead of the true form of these realities, it can never, by the same sacrifices that are continually offered every year, make perfect those who draw near.
> …Consequently, when Christ came into the world….
> Hebrews 10:1, 5

But Hebrews, like the other Epistles, is not a discourse in abstract theology. These truths about Jesus are very practical, that is, they are to be applied by Christians. What is the application that runs throughout the book? It is that those who profess Jesus must remain faithful to him through all trials and testing. This is called *perseverance*. Those who trust in Jesus, the fulfiller of shadows, prove their faith by remaining faithful to him in this life.

Exhibit A in this lesson is Israel wandering in the wilderness for forty years. God did not allow these unbelieving Israelites to enter the promised land of Canaan, a picture of spiritual rest or, more simply, of salvation. The unbelieving Israelites did not persevere in faith. The wilderness was their time of testing and they failed the test. The result: "They shall not enter my rest" (Hebrews 3:11).

So what is the lesson for you?

> Take care, brothers, lest there be in any of you an evil, unbelieving heart, leading you to fall away from the living God. But exhort one another every day, as long as it is called "today," that none of you may be hardened by the deceitfulness of sin. For we have come to share in Christ, if indeed we hold our original confidence firm to the end.
> Hebrews 3:12-14

Unbelieving Israelites not entering Canaan foreshadowed those who profess Jesus but do not persevere in faith and enter into spiritual rest. Merely participating in a church or identifying yourself as a Christian no more guarantees salvation than a Jew participating in the Exodus and wilderness wanderings was guaranteed an inheritance in the Promised Land. Faith is required to enter spiritual rest just as it is required to obtain the spiritual food described by Jesus. Faith is the spiritual prerequisite for spiritual food and spiritual rest. Both of these describe aspects of salvation in Jesus.

The great rest passage concludes with these words:

> For if Joshua had given them rest, God would not have spoken of another day later on. So then, there remains a Sabbath rest for the people of God, for whoever has entered God's rest has also rested from his works as God did from his. Let us therefore strive to enter that rest, so that no one may fall by the same sort of disobedience.
> Hebrews 4:8-11

Physical Canaan illustrates spiritual rest but it is not spiritual rest. There is "another day later on." The Old Covenant Sabbath pictures spiritual rest but it is not the thing itself. "There remains a Sabbath rest." The spiritual fulfillment of rest is found in Jesus, just as he said, "Come to me, all who labor and are heavy laden, and I will give you rest" (Mt 11:28).

Does Jesus' spiritual fulfillment of rest eliminate the need for physical rest? No, just as his spiritual fulfillment of food and marriage does not prohibit the physical expressions that we enjoy. Acknowledging the spiritual reality of these things does not require you to deny yourself the physical partaking of them. They are complimentary not antagonistic.

You may think that I am rather long-winded to make such an obvious point.

I was actually thinking that.

As I suspected. But I doubt that you are fully convinced to re-label your buckets...yet.

But...Jesus Is My Rest

As I have been writing this theology of rest, I have been talking with others to test my ideas and see how they are received. To my satisfaction most people have been interested in the topic. Rest is a fact of life, after all, and cannot be ignored. Each person *must* be a rest theologian, whether he wants to be or not, and must form his own thoughts and practices on the subject. Unfortunately, everyone is pretty much on his own. Rest is rarely taught or preached in our churches. With all of the confusion and controversy, apparently it is better to let sleeping dogs lie. So when I turn on the faucet, there is a lot of pressure built up and people are eager to talk.

In most cases, usually when I start describing my cabin rest, I will be interrupted with this protest: "But Jesus is my rest!" I hope that the person is saying, "Jesus is my spiritual rest, my salvation, my eternal life. I have faith in him and will receive this rest." Unfortunately, I realize that something else is being expressed, which is: "You are so *unspiritual!* All of this talk of reading and hobbies and cabins—shame on you! You ought to be encouraging me to do *spiritual* things." In other words, a person will usually admit that the concept of rest is right but protest that only certain types of rest activities are sanctioned for Christians. Cabins do not belong on the approved list, as well as many other activities that I recommend.

This person—actually I'm talking about *you*—is holding tightly onto buckets labeled "spiritual" and "unspiritual" or the associated labels.

Pillar Spirituality

Your labels are nothing new. These have been the majority labels in the Church for much of history. Consider, for example, the 4th and 5th centuries. The champions of spiritual/unspiritual labels at that time were the monks and hermits.

These fellows were serious about their labels. Some lived in tiny cells, subsisted on grass, deprived themselves of sleep, and frequently starved themselves for days on end. One of their champions was Simeon Stylites (circa 390-459 A.D.), who lived atop a pillar for thirty-nine years and was reported to have touched his feet with his forehead 1244 times in succession and to have "dripped with vermin." He maintains the record for pillar sitting, as testified to in the *Guinness World Book of Records*. No danger of being distracted by "unspiritual" activities on that pillar! He could devote full time to repressing his earthly affections up there. If I were more judgmental, I would say that Simeon may have been aiming at spirituality but hit idleness dead center instead. But I must be cautious because I am obviously in the theological minority on this one. Simeon Stylites has been commemorated as a saint by the Orthodox and Catholic Churches. In his day he and his fellow ascetics were known and admired as "athletes of God."

I will commend these hermits for one thing—the consistency between their theology and their practice. If you believe that physical life and material things are ultimately worthless, go all the way to deprive yourself of them. If you believe that only certain activities are eternally valuable, like self-denial, sell out all the way.

But the danger is that if this theology is wrong, you could end up on a pillar for no good reason. I bet Simeon yearned to do a good week's work instead of depending on the charity of poor shepherds for his food. And on Sunday afternoon, I bet he craved a little football and some buffalo wings, which would have brought him some needed refreshment.

Simeon Stylites extreme asceticism was driven by much more than an academic debate over the nature of spirituality. It was built upon a certain understanding of—or more pointedly, a hatred of—the physical aspects of earthly life. This despising of the physical world, including the body, is the theological root that causes deep confusion over how you should understand and live your life. This error predated the spiritual/unspiritual buckets of our day, the secular/sacred buckets of Luther's day, and even the pillar-sitting spirituality of the hermits. This error in its earliest Christian form is referenced in several of the Epistles, including this letter from Apostle Paul to Timothy:

> Now the Spirit expressly says that in later times some will
> depart from the faith by devoting themselves to deceitful
> spirits and teachings of demons, through the insincerity of
> liars whose consciences are seared, who forbid **marriage**
> and require abstinence from **foods** that God created to be
> received with thanksgiving by those who believe and know
> the truth. For everything created by God is good, and
> nothing is to be rejected if it is received with thanksgiving,
> for it is made holy by the word of God and prayer.
>
> 1 Timothy 4:1-5

The larger context of this passage is Paul's treatise on godliness or faithful Christian living. In this passage he addresses two physical aspects of life, that is, marriage and food. The ungodly (those who have departed from the faith) forbid marriage and abstain from certain foods. The godly receive these good physical gifts from God with thanksgiving.

To state the obvious, Paul does not commend asceticism here. He does not say it is the path to a higher spirituality. He does not identify it as criteria for canonization. No. He condemns these actions of physical self-denial in the strongest of terms. Why? Because godliness is not obtained by repressing, escaping, denying or mystically transcending the physical world.

These ideas are integral to other religions and philosophies but have no place in Christianity. Godliness is expressed in and through our physicality, not in spite of it. Faithful Christians glorify God in every aspect of life. If you want a model of godliness to emulate, I do not recommend the isolation and physical repression championed by Simeon Stylites. I recommend the everything-whatever spirituality displayed throughout the Bible by all of those who have honored God through their lives.

Wholly Holy

And what does this hysterical raving about asceticism have to do with rest? Are you implying that this somehow applies to me and my practice of rest? How dare you judge me…you…you Cabin Man!

Don't get mad at me. If the shoe doesn't fit, don't put it on. After all, you have no desire to become a monk or a nun or spend the remainder of your days atop a pillar, do you? You are married (or wish to be) and eat well. So far, so good.

Perhaps you only have a mild case of asceticism not the full-blown disease. You do not shun all earthly attachments, only certain ones—particularly ones concerning rest. This does not mean that you are not an ascetic. It just means that you are not a very good one. You may not have the conviction to become an "athlete for God," but you are at least able to muster up a little guilt over those rest activities that end up in your Ultimately Worthless bucket. That label—*Ultimately Worthless*—is the symptom that reveals the disease.

Let me repeat the Apostle Paul once more. "…**everything** created by God is **good**, and nothing is to be rejected if it is received with thanksgiving, for it is made **holy** by the word of God and prayer." This passage is most easily understood by contrasting it with the Old Covenant. Under Mosaic Law only certain things were to be considered as holy or set apart for God's service. Holy things were particular places (the tabernacle, the temple), professions (priests), objects (the ark of the covenant, ceremonial items used in sacrifice and worship), times (Sabbath, feasts and other sacred days), and people (the nation of Israel).

The New Testament teaches that these things were a foreshadowing of what would be fulfilled under the New Covenant. The Apostle Peter piles on this theme and says that everyone who believes is part of the nation (a holy nation), the priesthood (a royal priesthood) and the temple (living stones) that is holy. And so….

> …but as he who called you is holy, you also be holy in all your conduct, since it is written, "You shall be holy, for I am holy."
>
> 1 Peter 1:15-16

New Covenant holiness is inclusive of *all* of life—all your conduct, everything, everywhere. All is to be holy, set apart for the glory of God.

This includes all that you are, all that you do, and all that you have.

This truth should revolutionize your view of rest (as well as work). It should cause you to revise your theology. It should compel you to re-label your buckets to the biblical categories of work and rest. It should free you to partake and enjoy the many expressions of rest that will bring you refreshment.

CHAPTER ELEVEN

Worldly Earthly Fleshyness

I have been digging up the roots of your bucket mis-labeling. The three remaining roots are, perhaps, the deepest and most difficult to remove of all. Unless these are chopped away, I doubt that you will ever categorize your activities as work and rest.

You are wearing me out. Is this really necessary?

I think so. What is at stake is your joyful freedom to rest.

Let's dig in. How do you understand these three New Testament words: world, earth and flesh? These words describe physical things—the entire physical realm, the physical planet and your physical body.

There are two major interpretations of these words. The first is that world, earth and flesh are inherently evil, opposed to Jesus, and destined for judgment. The second is that these things are the objects and beneficiaries of Jesus' redemptive work. Which is it? Or is it both? Or is it neither? And how can this be reconciled with the New Covenant everything-whatever principle and concept of wholly holy holiness?

These are difficult questions. Before I share my thoughts, clarify your own position by taking the following quiz. Check one box to the right of each term.

	Negative Opposed to Jesus Judge it!	Positive Objective of Jesus Redeem it!	Both	Neither
World				
Earth				
Flesh				

If the terms are always used negatively—opposed to Jesus, as many Christians have held—then everything associated with the world, the earth and our flesh *should* be despised. You should repress your body not rest it. You should only desire the day when you are at long last free from this accursed physicality.

If this turns out to be the case, I will regret that I was not a little more positive about pillar sitting, and I will owe Simeon Stylites a big apology. On the other hand, if world, earth and flesh are used positively—as objects of Jesus' redemption—then there will be no conflict with the everything-whatever principle and the concept of wholly holy holiness.

It is time to test theological theory against biblical text. I will examine each term separately. The passages cited are a representative sampling of their New Testament usage. The first term is "world."

World (Greek—*COSMOS*)

Negative Use	Positive Use
Now is the judgment of this **world**; now will the ruler of this **world** [Satan] be cast out. (Jn. 12:31) If you were of the **world**, the **world** would love you as its own; but because you are not of the **world**, but I chose you out of the **world**, therefore the **world** hates you. (Jn. 15:19) Jesus answered, "My kingdom is not of this **world**. If my kingdom were of this **world**, my servants would have been fighting, that I might not be delivered over to the Jews. But my kingdom is not from the **world**." (Jn. 18:36) Has not God made foolish the wisdom of the **world**? (I Cor. 1:20) And you were dead in the trespasses and sins in which you once walked, following the course of this **world**, following the prince of the power of the air, the spirit that is now at work in the sons of disobedience—among whom we all once lived in the passions of our flesh, carrying out the desires of the body and	For God so loved the **world**, that he gave his only Son, that whoever believes in him should not perish but have eternal life. For God did not send his Son into the **world** to condemn the world, but in order that the **world** might be saved through him. (Jn. 3:16-17) Again Jesus spoke to them, saying, "I am the light of the **world**. (Jn 8:12) The God who made the **world** and everything in it, being Lord of heaven and earth, does not live in temples made by man.... (Acts 17:24) ... in Christ God was reconciling the **world** to himself.... (II Cor. 5:19) Of this you have heard before in the word of the truth, the gospel, which has come to you, as indeed

Negative Use	Positive Use
the mind, and were by nature children of wrath, like the rest of mankind. (Eph. 2:1-3)	in the whole **world** it is bearing fruit and growing…. (Col. 1:5-6)
See to it that no one takes you captive by philosophy and empty deceit, according to human tradition, according to the elemental spirits of the **world**, and not according to Christ. (Col. 2:8)	The kingdom of the **world** has become the kingdom of our Lord and of his Christ, and he shall reign forever and ever. (Rev. 11:15)
Do you not know that friendship with the **world** is enmity with God? (Jms. 4:4)	
Do not love the **world** or the things in the **world**. If anyone loves the **world**, the love of the Father is not in him. For all that is in the **world**—the desires of the flesh and the desires of the eyes and pride in possessions— is not from the Father but is from the **world**. (I Jn. 2:15-16)	

Hmmm. There is both positive and negative usage of the term. In the left column we see the physical world identified with Satan's influence—he is the "ruler of this world"—and the sinful inclinations of fallen humanity. However, in the right column it is clear that God loves the world and Jesus is its light. And while Jesus clearly stated that his kingdom was "not of this world" two thousand years ago, we learn that it will be in the end when "the kingdom of the world has become the kingdom of our Lord and of his Christ." On the left is the fallen, corrupted world. On the right is the world as God's creation, the world in the process of being redeemed, and the future fully redeemed world.

Closely related to the word "world" is the word "earth." Do we see this same pattern?

Earth (Greek—*GE*)

Negative Use	Positive Use
Their end is destruction, their god is their belly, and they glory in their shame, with minds set on **earthly** things. (Phil. 3:19)	Blessed are the meek, for they shall inherit the **earth**. (Mt. 5:5)
Set your minds on things that are above, not on things that are on **earth**. (Col. 3:2)	Your kingdom come, your will be done, on **earth** as it is in heaven. (Mt. 6:10)

I thank you, Father, Lord of heaven |

Negative Use	Positive Use
Put to death therefore what is **earthly** in you: sexual immorality, impurity, passion, evil desire, and covetousness, which is idolatry. (Col. 3:5) But if you have bitter jealousy and selfish ambition in your hearts, do not boast and be false to the truth. This is not the wisdom that comes down from above, but is **earthly**, unspiritual, demonic. (Jms. 3:14-15)	and **earth**…. (Mt. 11:25) I will give you the keys of the kingdom of heaven, and whatever you bind on **earth** shall be bound in heaven, and whatever you loose on **earth** shall be loosed in heaven. (Mt. 16:19) And Jesus came and said to them, "All authority in heaven and on **earth** has been given to me." (Mt. 28:18) The God who made the world and everything in it, being Lord of heaven and **earth**, does not live in temples made by man…. (Acts 17:24) …making known to us the mystery of his will, according to his purpose, which he set forth in Christ as a plan for the fullness of time, to unite all things in him, things in heaven and things on **earth**…. (Eph. 1:9-10) …and from Jesus Christ the faithful witness, the firstborn of the dead, and the ruler of kings on **earth**. (Rev. 1:5)

Just as with world, the earth (or the modifier form "earthly") is negatively identified with man's sinful desires and the influence of demons. It is also contrasted with "things above," that is, heavenly or spiritual things. But in the positive column, the earth has not been abandoned by God. In fact, it is clearly under the authority of Jesus' sovereign reign. Because of this, you are to pray that his kingdom comes to earth, which is the inheritance of the godly. And the earth is not contrasted with heaven, but united with it "in the fullness of time." The earth is the good creation of God, yet characterized by the fall, yet again the place of redemptive activity, and ultimately the kingdom of the redeemed under the Redeemer King.

There is one more word we must examine to complete the trio. That word is "flesh."

Flesh (Greek—*SARX*)

Negative Use	Positive Use
For while we were living in the **flesh**, our sinful passions, aroused by the law, were at work in our members to bear fruit for death. (Rom. 7:5) For I know that nothing good dwells in me, that is, in my **flesh**. (Rom. 7:18) Wretched man that I am! Who will deliver me from this body of death? Thanks be to God through Jesus Christ our Lord! So then, I myself serve the law of God with my mind, but with my **flesh** I serve the law of sin. (Rom. 7:24-25) For to set the mind on the **flesh** is death, but to set the mind on the Spirit is life and peace. (Rom. 8:6) But put on the Lord Jesus Christ, and make no provision for the **flesh**, to gratify its desires. (Rom. 13:14) Now the works of the **flesh** are evident: sexual immorality, impurity, sensuality, idolatry, sorcery, enmity, strife, jealousy, fits of anger, rivalries, dissensions, divisions, envy, drunkenness, orgies, and things like these. I warn you, as I warned you before, that those who do such things will not inherit the kingdom of God. (Gal. 5:19-21)	Father, the hour has come; glorify your Son that the Son may glorify you, since you have given him authority over all **flesh**, to give eternal life to all whom you have given him. (Jn. 17:2) For we who live are always being given over to death for Jesus' sake, so that the life of Jesus also may be manifested in our mortal **flesh**. (II Cor. 4:11) If I am to live in the **flesh**, that means fruitful labor for me. (Phil. 1:22) Now I rejoice in my sufferings for your sake, and in my **flesh** I am filling up what is lacking in Christ's afflictions for the sake of his body, that is, the church.... (Col. 1:24) ...for whoever has suffered in the **flesh** has ceased from sin, so as to live for the rest of the time in the **flesh** no longer for human passions but for the will of God. (I Peter 4:1-2)

The negative use of flesh is condemning indeed! It is directly equated with sin, both as an inward desire and an outward expression. It seems that there can be no good in the flesh...until we find some in the second column. Here you are exhorted to not only serve Christ in your flesh but even "manifest" him in your flesh. You perform "fruitful labor" and express the "will of God" through your flesh. Even more astounding, in a related passage, we learn that the Spirit of God indwells the flesh of a Christian: "Or do you not know that your body is a temple of the Holy Spirit within you, whom you have from God? You are not your own, for you were bought with a price. So glorify

God in your body" (I Cor.6:19-20).

So then, both major interpretations of world, earth and flesh are correct...in context. The negative use of these terms fully recognizes the fallen, sinful state of these physical things. In this state they are opposed to Jesus. However, the positive use reveals that these very things are also the object of Christ's transforming redemptive work. This work begins now and impacts every aspect of our present physical life. The transformation will be fully and completely realized upon the return of Jesus, who will make all things new, restored, perfected.

If you affirm both the negative and positive uses of these terms, you will be on balance. You will acknowledge the pervasive corrosion of sin *and* the restoring work of Christ in and through those he redeems.

As with most theological topics, however, distortion usually creeps in because of what you deny rather than what you affirm. If you deny either the negative or positive usages in order to preserve the logic of your theology, you will fall off of the beam into error. You will either make too little of this present physical world or make too much of it. Believe all that the Bible teaches and make sure that you do not deny something the Scripture affirms.

So here is how I grade the quiz:

	Negative Opposed to Christ Judge it!	Positive Objective of Christ Redeem it!	Both	Neither
World			X	
Earth			X	
Flesh			X	

How did you do? If you disagree with your score, submit your rationale to your pastor, an ombudsman, small claims court, arbitration or the academic dean. Or it might be easier just to improve your theology.

Are You Ready for Some Football?

Check the buckets. Mine are labeled as Work and Rest. Are yours still labeled as Ultimately Worthless and Eternally Valuable or have I persuaded you? Whatever the case, let us see how these two labeling classifications determine the value of football.

In my view, football goes into the Rest bucket if you are watching or playing it in order to refresh yourself from your work. If you play it professionally in order to earn your bread, it goes into the Work bucket. In either instance, the game itself is *not* spiritual because it is physical. It is a *seen* activity of the physical realm not an *unseen* activity of the spiritual realm. Football is of the world, of the earth and of the flesh.

A particular instance of football may be either sinful (negative) or God honoring (positive), depending on the obedience of the person involved in the activity. A man playing football may be playing for God's glory or he may be playing for his own. A man watching football may thoroughly enjoy a game, be refreshed from his work, and praise God for it. Another may spend the time cursing God in the frustration that all is not progressing as he thinks it should. He is less refreshed than when he started. Worse yet, he will have to kneel before Jesus during the final re-play when every action and thought will be fairly judged. It is the man and his faith or his lack of faith that makes the difference.

There is spiritual, unseen, and eternal significance to what occurs in a football game, but the game itself is not spiritual, just as no earthly activity is spiritual. Also, it is neither secular nor sacred, since these terms always make a false distinction under the New Covenant.

But the perspective on football is entirely different if your buckets are labeled as Ultimately Worthless and Eternally Valuable. Football is not thought of in terms of work or rest from this viewpoint. It simply belongs in the Worthless bucket with the other waste. Football is worldly, earthly and fleshly solely in the negative usage.

This is no problem if you do not like football, but if you do, your enjoyment of it is always diminished by regret. *I should have spent the time doing something better. I have failed to serve and honor God.* You are like the bulimic who eats some food and then, in remorse, pukes it out. No needed nourishment is gained from the food. In extreme cases, the bulimic will starve to death. In the same way your guilty conscience will rob you of the refreshment from a rest activity that you think is worthless.

You will still watch or play some football, most likely, because you need rest. But instead of giving thanks to God for it, you will perform penance through self-condemnation and repentance in order to evacuate what you feel was illicitly enjoyed.

Furthermore, you think football is *un*spiritual—or *against* the spiritual—because it competes for your time against "spiritual" activities, which in your theology are synonymous with religious activities. Or, if you prefer the other terminology, football is "secular" because it contrasts with what is sacred or holy—the things of this world set apart for God. The "spiritually mature" person, it follows, will forego football...and bowling and fiction reading and instrument playing and board games and movies and cabins.

The theology in both sets of labels is logically consistent with its definitions and assumptions, but they cannot both be right. It's one way or the other.

You know my recommendation: Work and Rest. But if you keep the Ultimately Worthless and Eternally Valuable labels on your buckets, you will remain more or less conflicted about most rest activities. The greater your conviction about these labels, the less you will rest well. This is the significance of the labels on your buckets.

CHAPTER TWELVE

Theology Complete

I began this theology of rest with a survey of the Scripture's teaching on rest. This teaching can be traced from the beginning to the end of the Bible. Although there was variation in the practice of rest, particularly between the Old and New Covenants, the main idea was really very simple. God rested from his work and so should you. Even if you do not agree on all particulars, you and I should be able to agree on this.

Every Christian should be a good rester, giving thanks to God for his gracious blessing. But most are not good resters. Most are guilty resters because there is something in their theology that spoils their rest. This, I suggest, is an unbalanced view of life in this world.

The key question is: What activities *can* glorify God? The New Covenant answer is whatever and everything, whether they are work or rest activities. This harmonizes beautifully with the way life really is or, to use my term, with the created order. Love and obedience to Jesus is expressed through all the things you do, not just through some of them.

This is true humanity, not an idealized spirituality that is as exhausting as it is impossible to achieve.

PART II

The Practical Theory of Rest

Theology behind and practice before,
There is much about rest left to explore.

What qualities comprise the basic characteristics?
How do you measure the essential statistics?

Jumpy distraction gives meager return.
The brain is unfocused, for good rest you'll yearn.

With work piled up, "No time for rest!" you declare.
In this assumption you do greatly err.

Ministry exhaustion gets you the highest of praise.
Idleness and rest are thought the same phrase.

Working for God—with this you're possessed.
But no rest with God is missing the best.

Where to begin? What misconception to kill?
Ah...let us sit at the feet of Mr. Churchill.

CHAPTER THIRTEEN

Painting with Mr. Churchill

Winston Churchill knew how to work well. He was one of the most productive workers in history. He was a war correspondent. He fought in four wars and led Britain through the greatest war of all—World War II. He served in Parliament over a period of sixty-three years. He held the following political and cabinet positions: President of the Board of Trade, Home Secretary, First Lord of the Admiralty, Minister of Munitions, Secretary of State for War, Secretary of State for Air, Chancellor of the Exchequer, and, for nearly ten years, Prime Minister. He was a powerful orator. He was a historian. He was a family man—married for fifty-five years and raised four children. He wrote fifty-six books and hundreds of articles.

How did he do it? Why didn't he crack under the strain? Why didn't he snap, explode, implode or collapse? You should know the answer by now. The man knew how to rest well.

No one could be such a prodigious worker without being an exceptional rester. He understood the relationship between the two and, more importantly, he understood the key to obtaining immensely refreshing rest. Fortunately for us he—being a man of words—wrote about it. His insight is captured in the little book *Painting as a Pastime*. The book was first published in the United States in 1950, but it was based upon two essays he wrote during 1921-22. The catalyst for his insight reaches back even further to 1915.

This was an extremely difficult time for Churchill. He had served as First Lord of the Admiralty for nearly four years—during the buildup to World War I and then in the thick of it. The strain of exertion is one

75

thing when you are winning but another when you suffer a disastrous loss. The loss was the Gallipoli Campaign, a joint British and French campaign to secure a supply route to Russia through the narrow Turkish straights known as the Dardanelles. Although Churchill was later officially exonerated, he was held politically responsible at the time. He resigned from the Admiralty and was essentially sidelined. He was worn out, miserable, depressed. His wife feared that he would die of grief. By coincidence, so to speak, he ran into his sister-in-law, who was painting. "I would like to do that," he said. And he tried it.

A Needed Change

Churchill was forty years old in 1915 and was already a pretty good rester. His not-work activities included an impressive list of hobbies, sports, games and other interests. But now he was at a greater level of exhaustion and required something with greater restorative power. That activity was painting, and it refreshed him through the remainder of his life, through even the more turbulent waters of World War II.

What was it about painting that he found so rejuvenating? I will come to that, but first hear what he has to say about resting in general. I will allow the man to speak for himself…because he does it so well. He begins *Painting as a Pastime* with these words:

> Many remedies are suggested for the avoidance of worry and mental overstrain by persons who, over prolonged periods, have to bear exceptional responsibilities and discharge duties upon a very large scale. Some advise exercise, and others, repose. Some counsel travel, and others, retreat. Some praise solitude, and others gaiety. No doubt all these may play their part according to individual temperament. But the element which is constant and common in all of them is Change. Change is the master key.[2]

Churchill identifies three pairs of opposites. Here they are once more:

---

[2] Winston S. Churchill, *Painting as a Pastime* (Cornerstone Library Publications: Pocket Books Inc., 1950), p. 7.

exercise—repose
travel—retreat
solitude—gaiety

Consider the first pair. The rest you require may be in the form of exercise, physical activity, or repose, physical inactivity. Here is welcome news.

One of the greatest misconceptions about rest is that it is synonymous with physical *in*activity. This is rooted in theological error, of course. Remember that the Mosaic Law prohibited *work* during Sabbath. It did not prohibit all physical activity. This is an important distinction.

The Old Covenant Jew was to observe Sabbath on the seventh day and during the feasts, festivals and other holy days. He was required to participate in the ceremonial observances, of course, but as long as he did not work during the remainder of the time he was also free to do as he pleased. This was what was stipulated in the written Law, the Torah. However, the Jews extrapolated and added to the written Law in an attempt to carefully distinguish Sabbath keeping from Sabbath breaking. One extrapolation, for instance, was defining how far one could walk on the Sabbath. This was known as a Sabbath day's journey (Acts 1:12). Rules like this equated physical exertion with work, instead of the biblical distinction of equating earning your bread with work. This restricted a Jew's options for Sabbath rest activities. He would violate his misguided conscience if he took a long, refreshing walk on the Sabbath.

Many Christians have faithfully carried on the error, misunderstanding both our freedom under the New Covenant and the nature of rest.

Boys Will Be Boys

This misunderstanding has been particularly hard on boys. Imagine the tortured youth who has been forced to sit quietly—angelic like—through Sunday school and church. Now he is ready to burst. When he arrives home, however, he is told that he must faithfully observe the "Sabbath" in certain ways—in prayer, reading and quiet contemplation, for instance. If he falls asleep and takes a nice little nap, that is fine too.

Is this is the rest that a boy yearns for? No, this is not rest for him. Torment, yes. I say, let the boy rest through the activities he naturally gravitates to—vigorous, active play and adventure. For him this is true refreshment. I wonder how many boys have soured on Christianity because they mistakenly equate the practice of it only with repose and never with exercise.

Then there is the area of schooling, which consumes much more of the unfortunate boy's rest-inhibited life. Here he is forced to sit quietly—compliant, passive, attentive, girl-like—hour after hour trying to digest information only for the purpose of regurgitating it during a test.

What rest does he get from this agonizing brain work? Recess, of course. When I was a boy recess meant going outside and getting in a good fight. Or, if you did not want to participate directly, you could cheer on one of the combatants or the other, which was safer, especially for me since I was a runt. But whether through direct involvement or vicarious participation the activity served to blow off some steam. Very rejuvenating. Very effective rest, although frowned upon by the authorities…and perhaps questionable for other reasons.

Less stimulating but still effective rest activities included tetherball, soccer, flying paper airplanes or anything else that required motion. Nowadays—from what I've heard—recess sounds more like a group therapy session focused on conflict resolution rather than the frenzied, joyful and restful chaos of yesteryear. How do boys get the active rest they need in such a controlled and tame environment? They don't. And to ensure they won't get much of it during the evening either, they are loaded up with homework. Perhaps this is why so many boys get frustrated, rebel and then are often drugged into compliance. But I have now needlessly drifted into another controversy.

I'll say!

To return to point, it is not only boys that require exercise rather than repose as a rest activity. Anyone whose work is not physically demanding should consider some type of exercise as a means to obtain rest. This includes more and more of us—cubical dwellers, meeting sitters, computer screen gazers, number crunchers, talkers, writers. On the other hand, those whose work is manually strenuous should consider activities where the body is in some state of repose, or inactivity.

The Bricks

Now stay with me for a moment. I'm going to work up something here.

When the queen of Sheba visited King Solomon she took note of all of his words. There was nothing that he could not explain to her. He was a good talker. But that was not what really impressed her.

> And when the queen of Sheba had **seen** all the wisdom of Solomon, the house that he had built, the food of his table, the seating of his officials, and the attendance of his servants, their clothing, his cupbearers, and his burnt offerings that he offered at the house of the LORD, there was no more breath in her.
>
> 1 Kings 10:4-5

It literally took her breath away when she saw how he put things into order. Here was wisdom fully expressed. So too, I could not fully appreciate Churchill's rest wisdom until I saw it physically displayed.

I saw it when I visited Chartwell, his country estate, south of London. One thing immediately caught my attention—all of the bricks. There are thousands of bricks at Chartwell. You walk on them. They form the fences and retaining walls. They are everywhere. Churchill built them all. "Bricklayer" probably does not come to mind when you think of Churchill, but he was one.

When Churchill was able to spend substantial amounts of time at his beloved Chartwell, when he was between major governmental responsibilities, his daily routine usually consisted of three parts: writing in the morning, brick laying in the afternoon, and entertaining in the evening. Writing was his work. This was how he earned his bread. Writing is intensely draining brain work, as any serious writer will tell you. To recover from the exertion he required a change, so he mortared bricks together. His daily pace was two thousand words and two hundred bricks. I do not know much about brick laying, but I do understand the mental effort behind writing two thousand words. Could he have written more words if he had not been playing around with the bricks? Or better words? I don't think so. His brick rest did not distract from his word work. His brick rest provided the change that enabled his word work.

Imagine if Churchill's work was not word writing but brick laying.

79

Say that he earned his bread as a mason. Could he obtain rest from his work by laying more bricks? Of course not. This would not be refreshing to him. More physical work does not provide refreshment for the same physical work. It provides exhaustion. But imagine again if Churchill the mason loved to write after a hard day of manual labor. Writing would be the change, the rest, he required. Words and bricks are very different activities. The first is primarily mental. The second is primarily physical. Doing one is a change from doing the other. "Change is the master key." That is why exercise will be appropriate rest for some, and why repose will be fitting for others.

With or Without Others

I will continue with Churchill's pairs of opposites.

The second is travel-retreat. For some the newness and excitement of travel will be the prescribed rest. For others the calmness and quietness of retreat will be just what is needed.

The third pair is solitude-gaiety. This is more simply stated as being alone versus being with others. Some are recharged in the first way, others in the second. I am sure Churchill was not attempting to be exhaustive in his examples, but these three pairs do pretty well characterize the main features of various rest activities.

So what makes one activity more fitting than another? Churchill says that it is "individual temperament." We more commonly use the term "personality." You are a combination of innate features and experiences that make you who you are. Needless to say, you are unique, which means that your rest must also be unique. Temperament or personality is most evidently expressed in the last pair of opposites. Do you prefer to rest in solitude (alone) or in gaiety (with others)? You need to understand yourself in this area. What refreshes others may not refresh you. This self-knowledge will guide you in selecting effective rest activities.

What is Happening?

There is another factor that plays upon your choice of rest activities in addition to individual temperament. This is present circumstances. The circumstances of life are not static. Each day brings new details, which are never quite the same. If circumstances result in a new or unusual type of work, then a new rest activity will be needed.

For example, you may be a very social person and understand that you are usually rested by getting together with family and friends. But you may have had a traumatic event in your life, such as the loss of a spouse. For weeks or months you have been fully absorbed in your spouse's illness, hospital, hospice, then death. You have been constantly surrounded by family and friends. In this case, rest may be needed in the form of repose, retreat, solitude—the opposites of what generally refresh you.

Life is in motion. Each type of work will require the appropriate corresponding rest. Solomon knew this. Once, when taking a break from trying to impress the Queen of Sheba, he said,

> For everything there is a season, and a time for every matter under heaven."
>
> Ecclesiastes 3:1

The one constant, though, is that rest must be a change from work if it is to bring refreshment. Remember that the most basic biblical definition of rest is not-work. "A change from work" is simply another way to say not-work. Change = not-work. Or, more fully, change = activities that refresh you after your work.

Lunch Break

Let me open my life for examination here. I earn my bread as a manager, which means I do a lot of interacting with people in one form or another. I know that I need rest from this work. I get tired of talking, listening and writing to people. I need to step away from this. I need a change, which for me means a little solitude. I find it during lunch. I go to an empty table in the break room and eat and read. Alone. The people I work with understand this and, for the most part, leave me undisturbed. When lunch is over, I am ready to re-enter the land of the living and re-engage humanity. I have obtained rest and am recharged. I am able to work hard the rest of the day.

However if I had a different job—say I was an engineer or software programmer—and my work took place mostly inside my own head, hopefully I would seek human interaction during lunch by some activity such as card playing, which some people do in the break room. I could give many other examples but the point is that "change is the master key."

In sum, to understand the type of rest that will truly refresh you requires an understanding of your work, your temperament, and your present circumstances. Good rest begins with a little self-awareness. This does not require deep introspection or professional therapy. It is really very simple. Just ask yourself this question when you are tired from work: *If I could do anything I wanted to do right now, what would it be?* What you enjoy doing will be a *change* that refreshes.

His Needs, Her Needs

But only if rest were so simple! If it only involved ME! It doesn't...unless you are Simeon Stylites. For most there are complications. Other people are the complications. And the closer they are, the more complicated the situation becomes. Most of the time I can get away with telling people at work to "buzz off" during my lunch break, but I should never tell my family at home to "get lost." *I need some solitude...so beat it!* Not wise. This will bring results, but it won't be refreshment. It will be something much less pleasant. My need for rest must be balanced with my responsibilities to others. So must yours.

Consider the scenario of a young married couple with a two-year-old and an infant. His work takes place in a cubicle and consists of politely talking to as many irate people as possible in eight hours in order to settle their insurance claims. Her work takes place in the home and consists of changing diapers, wiping regurgitation off of herself, and making goo-goo sounds all day long like a crazy woman. He returns home at the end of a tiring day. He needs rest. Her tiring day has been at home. She needs rest. Rest for each of them involves *change* from their work.

The problem is that each one needs change that appears to be opposite from the other's. She has been looking forward to the evening so that she can relate to a fully-formed human being. She wants to talk, talk, talk to him. He has been looking forward to the evening so that he can watch the game in peace and quiet. She wants out of the house. He wants to stay in the house. She wants gaiety. He wants solitude. Uh-oh! Looks like there will be a little domestic tension tonight.

But there is time for rest—enough time for both of them if they use it wisely. I will give them a little advice.

The couple must come to grips with the reality that they are no longer living in the past, especially in those seemingly glorious college days. Now they are married and have two young children. They know this, of course, but the implications have not really soaked in. They do not realize that rest in this stage of their lives must take a different form. Their work is different, so their rest must be different.

The rest activities of their college days have formed an idealized glow in the minds of our rookie domestics. She remembers those long romantic talks together. He remembers painting large colorful letters on his bare chest and acting like a crazy man for the television cameras during sporting events. *Ah, those were the days!* But those days are past. They will just become more and more frustrated if they keep trying to re-create something from a former stage of life.

This is so hard for them to see but so easy for you, isn't it? Of course you are a real person and they are only figments of my imagination. Nevertheless, you should not feel too superior since you do the very same thing—attempt to duplicate pleasant rest experiences from some time in the past when your life was different.

Why do you have to get personal? Focus on them not me!

Their Needs

Okay. I'll continue with the imaginary people. The young couple needs to adjust their rest activities to the new realities of their situation. The new realities are the children. These little people cannot be ignored. Most rest will now have to be taken with the children present.

Indeed there is much not-work at home for father to enjoy. Being with his children, playing with his children, reading to his children is a change from his job. Wrestling with little Mr. Poopy Diapers is substantially different than talking to Big Mr. Poopy Mouth, who's new Corvette was just sideswiped by his teenager. Wrestling with little Mr. Poopy will provide refreshment after talking to Big Mr. Poopy.

But what about mother? Since she has been with the children all day, more time with the children will not be refreshing to her. This is the same thing as laying bricks…after laying bricks all day. Her husband's playing with the children will provide a needed break for her. Without having to service the constant demands of the children, whatever else she does will provide a measure of respite. Her primary work is caring for the children. When she is free to do other things, this is change for her.

Furthermore, since he has been sedentary in his little cubical all day and she has been cooped up in the house or apartment, it would be a beneficial change for both of them to get outside for a while. A nice walk in the park would be just the thing. Put the darlings in the strollers. Stretch out the legs. Now, amazingly, another dynamic occurs. The little terrors are quiet! They just look around at things or fall asleep as they are rolling along. This provides opportunity for conversation. As he relaxes, his unpleasant exchange with Mr. You-Know-Who earlier becomes a humorous anecdote that makes his wife laugh. She still wants to talk, of course, and now is the proper time. Very refreshing for both of them.

Finally, they should have regular "date nights." This rest will cost something but is well worth the price of a babysitter. Better yet, impose on Grandma and Grandpa again. Also, she should allow, even encourage, him to take a night out with the boys every so often. He should provide opportunities for her to spend time with her girlfriends. She can watch the game with him. He can play board games with her. This is called "loving" each other. It is providing for each other's rest needs. It honors God within a marriage.

This is such excellent advice I only regret that I did not give it to myself a few decades ago. It is nearly a crime against humanity that this book was not available sooner.

Now let us move on—at long last—to Mr. Churchill's paintings.

The Paintings

So when I was at Chartwell I noticed all of the bricks. The bricks are an enduring reminder that Churchill understood the importance of having a change from work. The second thing that convinced me of Churchill's rest wisdom was his studio. Here were many of his paintings. I admit that I did not particularly care for his style—bright, bold colors—but that is beside the point. Churchill found great restorative refreshment in painting those paintings. Why? Again, I shall let him speak for himself.

> Painting is complete as a distraction. I know of nothing
> which, without exhausting the body, more entirely absorbs
> the mind. Whatever the worries of the hour or the threats
> of the future, once the picture has begun to flow along,

there is no room for them in the mental screen. They pass out into shadow and darkness. All one's mental light, such as it is, becomes concentrated on the task.[3]

The key phrases are "entirely absorbs the mind" and "concentrated on the task." I have mentioned already that Churchill had varied and multitudinous rest interests. These all provided change for him and afforded a degree of refreshment. But the reason that he advocated painting is because it required his full attention.

If change is the essential nature of rest, then concentration is the measure of the intensity or refreshing power of rest. The more you are engrossed in a rest activity, the more refreshing that activity will be for you.

Painting focused Churchill's concentration. He thought of nothing else when painting. He did not plan the next counterattack against the Nazis, mentally rehearse his next speech, or prepare a political strategy. Painting was like a safe house, a refuge, a cabin, for him. Work could not intrude there. It could not enter his thoughts because he was fully occupied with the details, the shapes, the colors and the strokes involved in painting.

Pause and consider this for a moment. The idea that rest requires concentration seems odd at first. You intuitively know that work—productive work, at least—requires it. If you are too dull to grasp this concept, someone—probably your boss—will soon point it out to you.

Focus on your job!
Pay attention to what you are doing!
Think about it!

But it is not so self-evident that rest requires it. In fact, you assume that the opposite is true. You think that that if your work involves concentration then your rest must surely involve relief from concentration. Isn't *not* concentrating the change you require from concentration? Perhaps you have even said:

I've thought enough for one day.
I need to vegetate for a while.
I am going to think about nothing.

---

[3] Ibid., p. 31

Churchill did not underestimate your capacity for such foolishness. He anticipates it and responds.

> The mind keeps busy just the same. If it has been weighing and measuring, it goes on weighing and measuring. If it has been worrying, it goes on worrying. It is only when new cells are called into activity, when new stars become the lords of the ascendant, that relief, repose, refreshment are afforded.[4]

He is more eloquent than I. I would simply say that you can only stop thinking about one thing (work) when you begin thinking about another thing (rest). Your brain train will continue down the same track until you switch it to another line. It is simply impossible not to be on a track, to think about nothing. If you do not believe me, try it. Think about nothing. When you have done this, move on to the next paragraph.

Did you think about nothing? No, you did not. You thought about thinking about nothing, which is thinking about something. And then, after about five seconds, you thought about moving on to this paragraph, which you did. So now try this. Think about your favorite flavor of ice cream. Recall a particularly pleasant memory when you were enjoying that ice cream. Can you see it? Can you almost taste it and feel the coldness? Can you remember who you were with at that moment?

Okay, come back. I'm losing you. The point is that when you start thinking about a new subject you are no longer thinking about the old subject.

But Churchill's main point is not so much the fact of our thinking about either one thing or the other but about the depth of our thinking. Thinking about work must be replaced with thinking about something else *and* thinking about it very intensely. By concentrating your thoughts on rest activities you are able to cease thinking about work, which is a continuation of work, and start thinking about something other than work, which is entering rest.

This concept is easy enough to grasp in theory, but putting it into practice is becoming increasingly difficult. Why? Well, this subject requires its own chapter.

---

[4] Ibid, pp. 7-8

CHAPTER FOURTEEN

Unconcentrating

Most members of the human race are not distinguished by having great powers of concentration. Even those few geniuses who amaze the rest of us with their uncanny ability to focus their mental energies on a particular subject or problem, seem to have little concentration left for the more mundane things in life, like zipping up their pants before leaving the restroom. Alas, this is the human condition.

This struggle to concentrate has been with us throughout history, but I am quite sure that it is getting worse. If I am right, then people are having an increasingly difficult time resting well.

If I have not yet offended you somewhere in this book, your turn may now have arrived. You may reject what I am going to say and assume that I am a reactionary, a Luddite, a dinosaur, a romantic, impractical. You may even feel threatened or insulted. To soften the blow and reduce the shock, I will slowly ease into the subject. I request your patience.

Don't Know Nothing About History

You think that the particular stresses you face make life exponentially more difficult than ever before. Why? Because you interpret history from your particular vantage point. From where you stand, the challenges closest to you loom large, while those of past generations seem less imposing. But if you realized that your forefathers had to confront equally daunting obstacles to rest, you would take courage and face your own particulars better. Consider this, if Winston

Churchill could make time for rest, should you really think that it is out of reach for you? More significantly, do you think that it is too difficult to follow the example of the Lord Jesus with the demands that he faced?

But…but they lived in simpler times. The pace of life for me is frantic, overwhelming. I live in an unprecedented era of overload. I cannot concentrate. I cannot rest well in this crazy environment!

You prove my point.

You imagine an idealized past where a wholesome balance of work and rest were supported by a more relaxed, slower paced social structure—an agrarian setting, the Victorian era, or even the 1950s. But these past eras would lose their warm glow if you were transported back in time and actually experienced them. Given a choice, I'll bet that you would not trade your particular challenges for eighty hours of farm work a week or twelve-hour days in the factory. They had challenges. You have challenges. But just as your wise predecessors made time to rest in their circumstances, so can you.

Having said this, you must recognize that the challenges are not the same. Expressions of work and rest evolve, particularly as technology advances. Technology changes you because it changes the way you do things. Technology changes the way you live both physically and mentally. The impacts of physical changes are more obvious, but alterations to the way you think are less so. They sneak up on you. You do not think much about how you think.

To illustrate the influence of technology in general, consider an advance from yesteryear. Since it is a couple hundred years old, there should be no doubt or controversy about how this technology has changed life.

Choo-Choo Change

I am thinking about trains. Trains revolutionized both work and rest by making movement fast and affordable. A rancher in Dakota could send his cattle to market in Chicago or buy a tractor that had been made in Peoria. Or the family who wanted to go west to Oregon or California could do so by enduring a few days of rolling scenery in a railcar instead of several perilous months of dust eating in a wagon. Regarding rest, Kansas flatland farmers could vacation in the Colorado mountains in nice little cabins. Life was obviously different after mechanized transportation. It changed everything: industry, business, travel, politics, agriculture and war. Therefore it changed how people lived their lives. Specialization and manufacturing expanded. Wealth increased. Workers commuted. People moved. Families dispersed. Communities adapted to the new social structures and so did the churches that served them.

It was not long before transportation technology became personalized in the automobile. Soon nearly everyone had a car of their own. The influence of transportation technology expanded even more. A few worried about the larger impacts of these changes on family, community and, more recently, the environment. But most were so enamored with the evident advantages that they simply went along for the ride, so to speak.

In fact, it was—and is—nearly impossible to not go along for the ride. It takes much time and effort to resist a technology that has made a structural change in society. Regarding transportation, it is not practical for most people to walk or ride a horse to church, much less to the job or to Grandmother's house.

You Shape Tools, Tools Shape You

That is the way it is with all technological advances. They spread rapidly and replace the prior way of life—whether you like it or not. You could focus your time and energy on refusing to use these technologies, but I suggest this would only mean that you keep using older technologies that are less efficient and, increasingly, less available. If you are going to expend a lot of effort to make a point, make sure that it is an important one. You can do better than marginalizing your influence because you refuse to utilize the latest technologies.

Besides, people are made to invent things. You are made in the image of the Creator God, who himself designed all things. You reflect his image when you create something. Furthermore, inventions or technologies are never really new. They merely reflect some aspect of divine design already present in creation. The inventor is just crudely utilizing God's design. But even these humble efforts allow you to exercise better stewardship in your spheres of responsibility. In broad terms, technology advancement fulfills the dominion mandate of Genesis chapter one.

This is not to say that every application of technology is good and just. No. While trains and cars are not inherently good or bad, sinful or not, they may be utilized for either good or bad purposes. Like any tool, the virtue or vice of their use is determined by the intent of the user. A car may be used to rob a bank or to take an elderly woman shopping. As a Christian it is always your responsibility to use technologies for good, for Christ-honoring purposes, not evil ones.

But your stewardship responsibility is not limited to using technologies for good purposes. Wisdom requires more than that. You also need to be discerning about how technologies impact the way you live. These impacts are obvious when thinking about trains and cars, but they are not so clear when it comes to the latest technological innovations. These newest ones influence you more mentally than physically. They shape habits of the mind more so than habits of the body. So it is time to leave the trains behind. It is brains that I wish to examine. What is technology doing to the way that you think? To answer this, I want you to concentrate on your unconcentration.

Buzz Buzz! Beep Beep!

Concentration is the sustained focus of the mind. It is the preoccupation of thought on a single activity. It is persistent attention to something of interest. This is the sense in which Churchill uses it, as do I. Concentration is required for both productive work and refreshing rest. Unconcentration is the reverse state of mind. It is not an emptying of the mind or a focus on nothing, as I have discussed. It is rather a frequent switching of attention from one bit of stimulus to the next.

Is there some remote connection between technology and rest in all of this jabbering? You are wandering. You are distracted! Concentrate, Cabin Man!

I'll try. What technology most affects your ability to concentrate? It is your information technology—particularly computers, wireless communication and the combination of the two. Of course these technologies follow a long line of electronic advancements—the telegraph, the telephone, the radio, the television, and others. The new devices combine all of these functions—plus many new ones—into small machines that we can now carry in our pockets. Like mechanical travel, the technology has become personalized. Everyone has one of their own. I call them "gizmos." Because gizmos are always with you and you are always using them, they exert a very strong influence upon you. They shape the way you think.

I see where you are headed now. But gizmos, as you call them, have obviously expanded our powers of concentration. People are entirely focused on those little things. Haven't you noticed that?

Squirrel!

At first glance concentration appears to be a strength of the technology. What captures and holds someone's interest more than his gizmos? Look around. That boy is so completely mesmerized by a game that he might as well be on another planet. Perhaps he is. That teenager is so absorbed in explaining her travails to a friend that she is unaware that such personal details are inappropriate in a checkout line at the grocery store. That guy in the business meeting is so involved in reading his email and text messages that he is not hearing a word being spoken.

Did you notice that I equated "concentration" with "interest" in the above paragraph? I set you up, which was easy because you think that that these two terms mean the same thing. They do not. Interest is a broad category. Anything you pay attention to is something that you are interested in. If you were not interested, you would not bother to consider it at all. Your attention is always captured by what is most interesting to you at the moment.

But you do not concentrate on everything that you are interested in. The distinction is in the pace and depth of your thought. Concentration is when the pace is slow and the depth is deep. Unconcentration is when the pace is fast and the depth is shallow. Chess is an example of the first. Tic-tac-toe is an example of the second. Concentration initiates and explores. Unconcentration reacts. Concentration chews and savors. Unconcentration takes a quick bite and swallows. Concentration is Churchill focused on a painting. Unconcentration is his dog focused on a squirrel...and then a rabbit...and then a fly...and then a bone...and then a scratch behind his ear.

Gizmos train your mind to function like Churchill's dog. How? By providing a constant stream of changing stimulus that provides something new for you to be interested in—messages, calls, video, music, maps, data, documents, reminders, games. It is not the content so much that shapes your thinking, but the pace at which the content changes. *Read this. Make a comment to that. Watch this. Hear that. Do two things at once. No, do three or four things at once.* This constant mental switching forms the way that you think. You get mentally addicted to the rapid rate and variety of input and, as in any addiction, you must get more and more in order to achieve a buzz.

Television of Yesteryear to Rescue Camps

Think about the way old timers like me used to watch a televised football game. There is this angle and then this one and then a cheerleader and then a replay and then the commentator and then a commercial about trucks and then a commercial about beer and then a shot of the coach, etc. *Switch, switch, switch, switch, switch.* Worriers like me were concerned that so much rapidly switching stimulation might affect the capacity for sustained thought.

Perhaps it did. Just look at what happened to all those kids who were plopped in front of the television to watch *Sesame Street* every day. The educational programing was designed to captivate them and turn them into geniuses. *Switch, switch, switch, switch.* They were captivated all right, but instead of turning into geniuses they got bored by everything else. School was boring (I mean even more boring than it actually is). Family was boring. Life was basically boring. *Slog, slog, slog, slog.*

But all of that is old school already.

Now the football broadcast includes a stream of statistics, as well as highlights, to amuse you lest the game itself gets too boring. Or you may watch two games at once...or more. Better yet, watch football with your gizmo in hand. This raises the level of stimulus input to battlefield conditions. In addition to the game(s), you can text your friends while checking your fantasy league standing, your social media sites, the bargains, the news, the weather, and the latest amusing YouTube videos.

As for those would-be geniuses watching *Sesame Street*, they are multitasking too. While learning the letters of the alphabet they are also using their gizmos to perform rapid stock trades and are selecting their next rent-a-nanny. Do you think that is funny? Just wait.

But there is a price to be paid. And savvy entrepreneurs are willing to sell.

Hotels and resorts are beginning to tap into the market potential of exhausted gizmo-ites who long for an escape from electronic overload and are willing to pay for "digital detox" or "offline" vacations. Some of the weary will go to great lengths to find refuge in a remote wilderness or an undeveloped country of the world. They are seeking relief from constant mental switching. They are searching for a quiet place where they can find peace of mind, that is, where they can have sustained, uninterrupted thought. When such an elaborate escape is not possible, they may be compelled to take drastic action right at home—an "electronic fast" for a week or at least turn off their gizmo for the evening or weekend. But if the crisis cannot wait, they can check themselves into an increasing number of hospitals for treatment.

If adults are concerned about themselves, they are even more concerned about these powerful effects on their children. Kids become apathetic about things in the real world because they are too boring compared to the rapidly switching environment of their virtual world. In desperation their parents send them to "internet rescue" and "deprogramming" camps. This is not silliness or overreaction. It is a reasonable response to an addiction to gizmos and their impact on the mind.

And the connection to rest is....

Churchill said that concentration is an essential component of rest. He was right about that. Unfortunately common culture does not encourage this habit of mind. Instead of fostering attentiveness and prolonged focus, it reinforces distractedness, a rapid jumping from one thing to the next.

However, most of the blame for your jittery mental condition still falls on you. Why? Because you have diligently trained yourself to un-concentrate through the ever increasing use of your gizmos. The bottom line is that you are no longer concentrating on anything, including rest. When you do not concentrate on your rest, you do not rest well and do not become fully refreshed from your work.

What To Do?

I have already mentioned some approaches for finding relief from the relentless distraction of gizmos. These range from the desperate, such as deprogramming camps, to the mundane, such as turning off the gizmo at night. These may be categorized as "denial" activities. You determine *not* to use the gizmo or *not* to watch the television.

The drawback of denial is that you are focused on what you are trying not to do rather than what you would rather do. Diets are denial approaches. Most fail because you cannot stop thinking about what you are not eating. Eventually you will eat the food in your thoughts. Of course you will. And you will eat a lot of it. Just like you will binge on your gizmo after trying to go cold turkey.

When this approach fails, you can hire a psychiatrist. He will have a label for your condition, such as Internet Addiction Disorder (IAD). You have a disorder. That is why you cannot rest and are exhausted. You need professional treatment and, perhaps, drugs. Or you can take the economical route and self-medicate. Take some drinks to relax…or use other substances, let us say "non-prescriptions." The search for rest may lead you in many directions.

But I recommend neither denial nor drugs. I recommend *replacement*. Replacement is simply doing a new activity instead of an old one because you want to do the new one more than the old one. Your interest, desire, affection and commitment to the new activity becomes greater than what you have for the old activity. While this change of focus often begins with discontent for the old activity, your focus shifts to the pleasures and benefits of the new activity. This dynamic is repeated throughout the New Testament, as here:

> So then let us cast off the works of darkness and put on
> the armor of light. Let us walk properly as in the daytime,
> not in orgies and drunkenness, not in sexual immorality
> and sensuality, not in quarreling and jealousy. But put on
> the Lord Jesus Christ, and make no provision for the flesh,
> to gratify its desires.
>
> Romans 13:12-14

This command is negative and positive. Stop doing what is bad and start doing what is good. If you only go half way, the dirt will fall back into the hole. You must put something better in the hole, something that you will find greater delight in. This principle has far wider application than rest activities, but it includes rest activities.

The Gardening of Rest

Back to Churchill. When Churchill saw his sister-in-law painting he said, "I would *like* to do that." Painting initially captured his interest, and he thought that it would be something he could enjoy. His encounter with painting did not stop there or after a time or two of smearing paint on a canvas. He continued. The nature of the activity required learning and a development of his skill. That is, it required concentration.

Less effective rest activities, like weeds, grow by themselves and are less demanding. The best rest activities, like painting, require cultivation, like gardens. The more engrossed you become in the activity, the more interesting it becomes, the more you enjoy it, and the more refreshing the rest it provides. Then your affections are drawn to these activities so that they become the things you most desire to do.

And there is an important collateral benefit. By concentrating during rest you are training your mind to stop incessantly jumping around and start thinking deeply. If you do this enough, you will form a habit of mind that will also yield great benefit to your work. So concentration during rest benefits your work both directly and indirectly.

In the next section of this book I will recommend and describe several rest activities. I admit that these are my favorites, ones that most require my full concentration and, therefore, provide me the deepest level of rest. They may or may not be beneficial for you. I only hope to illustrate the benefit of intentionally nurturing these types of deep rest practices in your life.

But first I will consider several other aspects of the practice of rest.

CHAPTER FIFTEEN

No Time for Rest?

Do I sense increasing hostility? Some frustration that I have aggravated? Okay, out with it.

You can find time to rest in your Leave-It-To-Beaver world, but that's not my situation. I'm a single parent or working three jobs or going to school at night or am mostly on the road. And I don't have a nice little cabin in the mountains! What should I do? Where's the rest for me, you middle-class, Father-Knows-Best, comfortably-stable person?

Soooo…you don't like my examples? Don't fit, eh? That's fine. They are just illustrations. As I have said previously, each person's circumstances are different. Your circumstances are different than mine. Each of us is unique and must cultivate appropriate rest activities. This is self-evident, but it is not what you are mad about, is it? You are mad because you do not think that you have enough time for rest. You do not have time for a change from your work. This is the real issue and you have been waiting for an opportunity to unload on me and my idealistic rest theories. Okay. Unload. Get it all out in the open.

My life is too pressured, too packed, too chaotic to allow for proper rest. I cannot afford to not-work because I have too much work. I bear an exceptional weight of responsibility. I am a doctor, a counselor, a business owner, a CEO, an officer, a home-schooling mother of five. Others depend on me. Decisions cannot wait. Tasks must be done right now! I have no choice. As a result, exhaustion is my constant companion. This is my burden and I must bear it.

There is an issue here. If I do not deal with it now I will lose you.

Nobody Knows the Trouble I've Seen

To begin with, I do not doubt that your work burden is heavy, friend. Your work burden *should* be heavy. You should work long and hard. You must not be an idler, which is sin. You should work vigorously to fulfill your vocational callings and bring glory to God through them. I commend your work efforts…but I challenge your claim that you do not have time for rest.

You say that you cannot rest adequately and become fully refreshed. If this is true, everything in this book is wrong. It is wrong because my foundational premise is that God's created order consists of a work-rest cycle. If I understand this correctly, then there is enough time both for work and rest. But if you are an exception to the work-rest cycle, then I must be wrong about the created order. The created order, by definition, cannot apply to some people, some situations, and not to others. You cannot fashion your own personal created order anymore that you can fashion your own personal God. He is what he is. His created order is what it is. You can attempt to deny it and suffer the consequences of your foolishness, or you can live in harmony with it and enjoy its blessings. The choice is yours.

So why do you think that you do not have enough time to rest? There are three reasons. The first is that you have a misconception about the dynamics between work and rest. The second is that you do not *want* to be rested. The third is that you simply do not know how to rest well, which includes resting efficiently. I will deal with the first two in this chapter.

The Math of Work and Rest

In the first section of this book—the theology of rest—I wrote about the error of feeling guilty for resting because it is "unspiritual." Now I am exploring the practical matter of coping with the heavy press of life's demands. So many things to do. So little time to do them. You become so overwhelmed with work that you think you do not have anything left for rest. Your work burdens are so heavy and your responsibilities so great that you think that you cannot set them down, cannot take a good breather, and cannot enjoy activities that provide change.

You suppose that working hard is synonymous with resting little.

Rest must be minimized so that work can be maximized. Your underlying assumption is that the work-rest relationship is a zero-sum calculation. You subtract from one in order to increase the other. The more you work, the less you rest. The more you rest, the less you work. One hour of work can be traded for one hour of rest, like so:

$$\text{Time} = \text{Work} + \text{Rest}$$
so
$$\text{More Work} = \text{Less Rest}$$
or
$$\text{More Rest} = \text{Less Work}$$

I'll put actual numbers to the concept.

$$10 \text{ hours} = 8 \text{ of work and } 2 \text{ of rest}$$
or
$$10 \text{ hours} = 9 \text{ of work and } 1 \text{ of rest}$$

Obviously the diligent person works nine out of the ten hours. Obviously the…uh…let us say less diligent person works only eight. You want to be a diligent, productive, fruitful person, so you obviously should work more and rest less. This appears to be self-evident and irrefutable. Such overpowering common sense is based on the following assumptions.

$$\text{Work} = \text{Time Spent at Work Activities}$$

and

$$\text{Rest} = \text{Time Spent at Rest Activities}$$

But let's see if this holds up in real life.

Making Gizmos

Consider Jane who works on a production line accomplishing Step 432 of an assembly process that produces Super Gizmos. If Step 432 takes fifteen minutes to complete, Jane produces four units in an hour. In eight hours of work she will produce thirty-two units. By putting in an hour of overtime, she will produce thirty-six-four more units. So, from this perspective, she is a more productive worker when she works longer. Case closed.

Or is it? If a little overtime increases Jane's productivity, more overtime will make her even more productive, right? I'll incentivize Jane to work ten hours a day…no make that twelve or even fourteen. And we will increase her work week to six days from five…and all seven days every other week. Think of all of the units that Jane will be cranking out! And she will be getting richer with all of that overtime pay! Everyone will be a winner.

What a star Jane is! She becomes Employee-of-the-Month and gets the Employee-of-the-Month parking space. But after three months of such heroics, Jane does not feel like a winner. She feels lousy. She has big circles under her eyes. There is trouble at home. She is putting on weight, has no energy, and cannot seem to shake a cold. Her boss does not feel like a winner either. The line has been slowing down. Step 432 is taking three minutes longer than it should when Jane is working. This creates a bottleneck on the entire line and is impacting the profitability of the company. Fewer Super Gizmos are being produced. When the boss talks to Jane about picking up the pace, she blows sky high! *Do you realize how hard I am working? Do you know the sacrifices I make for this company?* This little drama attracts attention, of course, further lessening productivity.

The point is that even in a production line work environment more time spent working does not necessarily equal more work produced. There are limits. Without proper rest, the worker's work degrades and will become counterproductive at some point.

Further Disruption of the Work-Time Continuum

Anyway, it strikes me as an absurdity that business quality and productivity improvement theories are still based on a production line model such as this. Henry Ford, that great captain of the Industrial Age, still dominates our work imagination—stop watch in hand, eliminating wasteful motions, turning workers into efficient machines doing simple repetitive tasks, cranking out legions of Model Ts. How many of us actually work like this anymore…besides fast food employees? Not many. Last time I checked we had moved on to the Information Age or the Digital Age or whatever Age it is now. The main thing is that we have figured out how to make machines work like machines, while most of us humans get to use our brains on the job again.

The more a job consists of brain work, the less direct correlation it has to time. A complex project plan may take three hours or three months to construct, depending on the skill and expertise of the one creating it. Furthermore, the three-month plan may be completely unrealistic and cause significant inefficiencies in the project, while the three-hour plan may be right on the mark.

Question. Who is working harder in this scenario? Is it Billy, the enthusiastic college grad that is eating pizza at his desk at 8 p.m. and working through weekends while cranking out the three-month plan or Harold, the grizzled office fixture that slipped out early to go bowling after whipping out the three-hour plan?

It depends on how you calculate your work math. If the equations above are correct, then Billy is the harder worker because he is spending more time *at* work. He gets the Employee-of-the-Month parking place. But something seems amiss here. Isn't accomplishment a part of the equation? If it is, then the point of work is not to spend time *at* work but to produce something through work. It makes no difference if the something is Super Gizmos or insurance policy sales or raising children or ministry to the elderly.

Recalculating

Hmmm.

$$\text{Work} \neq \text{Time Spent at Work Activities}$$

The same holds true for rest. Just because you spend time on a rest activity does not automatically ensure that you will be refreshed from your work. You may not be refreshed at all. It may be ineffectual, just as time spent working may be ineffectual. You may even find yourself further exhausted. So the corollary to the above equation is:

$$\text{Rest} \neq \text{Time Spent at Rest Activities}$$

Back to work. Business owners and bosses know that an employee's presence does not equate to work being done. The good bosses, at least, focus on accomplishment. They do not fixate on overtime. A boss with this perspective will give the Employee-of-the-Month parking place to Harold, Mr. Grizzled Fixture—bowling excursion notwithstanding. He did the best work.

Those who have jobs in large organizations often lose focus on what the work product actually is. It is obscured by the complexities of bureaucracy. But you do not usually transfer these confusing work abstractions to your other vocational responsibilities. If a toilet at home is clogged, you do not reckon that you have been "working really hard" if you have spent twenty-seven hours on the task and the toilet is still backed up. You will most likely think that you have wasted a lot of time because you did not know what you were doing and that the work remains undone.

So a new equation is needed. Here it is.

$$\text{Work} = \text{Productivity}$$
$$(\ldots\text{and the corollary}\ldots \text{Rest} = \text{Refreshment})$$

This math is a game changer as to how you think about work (and rest). Your focus is changed from how much time you have spent working to what you have actually accomplished. How much you accomplish is related to how well you work. If you work well, you will have enough time for both work and rest. But if you do not work well, like Jane or Billy, you are more likely to skimp on rest and then take too much time to get too little work done. There is a dynamic here.

Reaping the Whirlwind

I call this the "Exhaustion Spiral." Here is how it operates in more detail. You cut short your needed rest initially in order to attempt to do more work. Now you become overly tired and your work suffers as a result. You cannot concentrate. You make mistakes. You are short tempered and offend others, leading to additional problems.

As a result, you have even more work to do, so you try to reduce your rest time even more. This only ensures that your rest is less effective because you feel guilty about resting with so much work piling up. The result is inferior resting. Guilty resting is lousy resting because you cannot fully concentrate on the activity. Your mind keeps jumping back to what work you think you should be doing. Lousy resting is less refreshing. Inevitably you end up with more time *at* work and getting less work done...and diminished refreshment from your rest. Here is the math from the perspective of time investment.

Productivity = Time *at* Work ÷ Inefficiencies (i.e. Tiredness & Stress)

Refreshment = Time *at* Rest ÷ Inefficiencies (i.e. Guilt & Distraction)

In each equation the effectiveness of work or rest activities is degraded by inefficiencies. Work is reduced by insufficient rest and, in return, rest is pressured by diminishing work productivity. One area negatively impacts the other. This becomes a downward, self-feeding cycle.

The Parent Trap

The Exhaustion Spiral is most obvious on the job but is just as true in the other areas of vocational responsibility.

Take parenting, for instance. Dedicated parents, supposedly, are the ones who fill up their evenings and weekends attending their children's activities and transporting them to and from these events. *I've gone to every one of Little Jimmy's soccer games this year.* Comments like this reap harvests of praise in our culture. The more time you spend *with* your children, the better parent you are...or so says the accepted wisdom. This is simply another venue of more time *at* work. Dedication to the children is measured by hours expended on the children's activities— sports, plays, science projects, musical recitals, and youth groups.

Careful! You're meddling now!

I know that you are under tremendous social pressure to do these things. And I am not saying that you should avoid all of them. That is not my point. At least some of these activities may be very beneficial to your children. I am only pointing out that many well-intentioned parents find themselves in an Exhaustion Spiral when they attempt to do everything that they think is expected of them.

Step back from it all for a moment. What really is the work of parenting? Is it keeping up with the Jones's? Is it providing your children a robust résumé? Well, wise parenting may involve many things depending on the abilities and giftedness of your children. But your primary objective is to "...bring them up in the discipline and instruction of the Lord" (Ephesians 6:1-4).

Parents need to be at the top of their game in order to accomplish this. Such a demanding task requires great love, discernment, perspective and patience. These are not usually the characteristics associated with haggard parents caught in a whirlwind of their children's activities, spending lots of time for little return and neglecting rest so that everyone is stressed out.

In the next chapter I'll talk more about working *and* resting with children. Here I am only pointing out that popular notions of parenting can quickly lead you into an Exhaustion Spiral, which makes parenting much more difficult.

Compound Interests

I have provided two examples of how more time *at* something does not necessarily mean more is getting done. Whether on the job or in the family, overtime usually results in less work being accomplished and insufficient time for rest. This is true in every one of your vocational responsibilities. I could provide more examples in hope of hitting your exact situation, but this is your work to do not mine. I am just trying to describe the dynamics of work and rest. I'll describe and you apply.

Before I conclude, though, let me bring what I have separated back together. I have examined the vocational areas of job and parenting in isolation. But things are not so simple real life. In real life all areas of your work push against each other. Every one of your vocational responsibilities competes against the others for your limited time.

I have not addressed that third major category of your vocational responsibility—ministry. Even if you agree with me concerning the relationship between work and rest in the areas of job and family, you probably do not think that it applies in the area of ministry. I will try to convince you otherwise, of course, but I will require a separate chapter to do it. Stay tuned for that. I will only point out now that ministry work contends for your limited, precious hours with the time allocated for earning your bread and caring for your family. And, like for these areas, greater time at work does not equate to more productivity. Neither does reducing rest.

Multiplication Not Subtraction

Now I will change the equation that I started with. Instead of simply measuring work as the time spent *at* work, I will measure the desired outcome of the work, i.e. productivity. Productivity is accomplishing the objective of the work, not merely spending time in pursuit of it.

You used to assume that rest time subtracted from work time, but this new perspective helps you to see the true dynamic between work and rest. Rest enables work. The better you rest, the better you work. The more refreshing your rest, the more productive your work. Rest is actually a multiplier of work. It is a multiplier because a good rest allows you to return to work re-charged, re-invigorated and renewed. A proper perspective is restored. Physical and emotional strength returns. Problems that seemed unsolvable become solvable. You try a different approach. A groundbreaking idea comes to mind. You confess your sinful outburst to a co-worker and restore cooperation. You confess the neglect or disrespect of your spouse and restore your marriage. You have an important talk with your kid.

The new math looks like this:

$$Productivity = Work \times Rest$$

So your objection that you do not have enough time for rest because you have too much work is based on a misconception of the relationship between work and rest. You cannot afford *not* to rest because rest is a multiplier of work. You will accomplish more work when you rest well. This revelation may help many of you break out of the Exhaustion Cycle. But some of you will not break out of the cycle…because you want to be in the cycle.

That's it, Cabin Man! You've really gone over the edge with this one! I don't want to be exhausted! That is ridiculous.

You object? Well, in order to evaluate this next concept, I'll say that this is not about you. It is about "those people." They will spring to mind as soon as I begin to describe them. I am sure that you never do it. No never. I'll shine the spotlight on them not you.

Simplifying Through Overwork

Those people remain in a condition of overwork and exhaustion for one very beneficial reason—it simplifies their lives. This is no small thing. Fulfilling your vocational callings—I mean "their" vocational callings—is a demanding task.

Consider the case of Mr. Buford. Buford works long hours on the job—fifty to seventy hours a week. Buford makes sure everyone, especially his boss, is aware of this. He is the first to arrive at the office and the last to leave. He sends emails on Sunday. What dedication! How hard he works! Such nobility! Uh-huh. In addition to admiration from his colleagues, Bufort gets a pass on all the work he does not do or does not do well. *It's no wonder Buford didn't get to that—he's already putting in overtime. Give that job to Jones.*

On the home front things are different. Buford expects to get a pass here too, but his wife does not give him one. *When was the last time we went out to dinner...the company holiday party?* His teenage daughter does not give him a pass either. *When did she dye her hair orange?* Even his ten year old son does not give him one. *Was that Cub Scout event last weekend or this weekend?* Buford is neglecting his vocational calling related to family. When his wife mentions the obvious, Buford gets upset. He insists that he deserves a pass. *I've got to work these long hours in order to provide for the family! I do it for you! You're so ungrateful.* Uh-huh.

Ditto for church involvement. Spending so much time on the job, where he is most comfortable, provides justification for not doing the more demanding work related to family and ministry. So he overworks at the job in order to avoid his other work. Exhaustion buys his excuse. This simplifies his life to a degree that he considers to be manageable. The mess it creates, of course, is not manageable, so he ends up seeking even greater refuge at the office. This behavior creates its own destructive cycle.

Simplifying Through Crisis

There is another version of this malady. It is less common but more extreme. Those people seem to travel through life lurching from one crisis to the next. They are always in some calamity or another—the car need repairs, lost the job, broke, betrayed, dumped, depressed, brother is in jail, mother is dying in Toledo. It is always something.

They never get a break. They are forced by these circumstances—as they would describe it—into a state of permanent exhaustion. And because of their exhaustion, they feel they have an excuse for ignoring their vocational responsibilities.

Those people also feel entitled to others' concern and help. Of course you see right through those people—they are self-centered, completely focused on their own problems. They demand that others focus on their problems too…constantly. They leverage their exhaustion and manipulate family, friends, and charitable persons. Exhaustion is their power and their excuse. If they became rested, they would lose both. They want to be in crisis. Why? Because life really is complicated. Because vocational callings are demanding—the difficult balance of jobs, family and church. Everything becomes simpler in a crisis.

When a real crisis hits, you understand when someone focuses on that one thing—the death in the family, cancer, a lost job—and ignore everything else. Everyone experiences a crisis now and then. Crisis legitimately draws your entire attention and others will understand and support you. They will also give you a pass when you set aside everything not directly related to the crisis. But when the crisis passes, you should rest to recover from it and then take up the yoke of your full responsibilities again. If you don't the crisis becomes an excuse for idleness, for not doing your work.

Overwork and crisis are just two examples of how you may justify neglecting your needed rest, but there are a thousand ways to do it. Your own technique is probably not as obvious as these. It is most likely subtler—perhaps cleverly disguised even from yourself.

But enough of this psychologizing, this staring into the abyss of self-deceit. Lift up your eyes! The Sovereign Lord, the God of Rest, knows your every thought and intention. Humble yourself. Seek him. Ask for wisdom. Confess when convicted. Set your heart to glorify him in all things—through a balance of work and rest.

CHAPTER SIXTEEN

What Am I Doing Under the Cabin?

By now you should have realized that this book is not mainly about cabins. It is mainly about resting. The title—*Buy a Cabin*—is a hook to catch your interest so that you will read the book. The hook works because "cabin" has pleasant associations—mountains, lakes, woods, peacefulness, apartness, simplicity, family and friends. In other words, you imagine that a cabin is a very fine place to rest. The mention of "cabin" draws your interest to the topic of rest.

But "cabin" is more than a mental image for me. I have a cabin, a wood-and-brick cabin, not merely an ideal of a cabin. This brings complications. Things do not always turn out the way I hope they will. Sometimes I have unrealistic expectations. Sometimes I am disappointed by the real-life experience. But not all of the time. Sometimes things are as good as or even better than I expect. My cabin has been that way for me...although not always in the way I anticipated.

The practice of rest at my cabin has sometimes surprised me. In fact, more than any other place, my cabin has become a rest laboratory, a place where I put my theories through rigorous test and evaluation. Will my musings survive the impact of reality? Or, more simply, will I actually be refreshed by my cabin experience?

Put Up or Shut Up

The complexities and struggles of reality began when I was deciding whether or not to buy a cabin. The process of writing this book, of thinking, led me to the conclusion that I needed to get serious about rest—serious enough to overcome my naturally frugal inclinations and make a major investment. That is always the way it is with rest—an investment is required. It always involves spending time. Sometimes it also involves spending money. Rest costs.

Being intellectually convinced that rest is important was one thing. Writing a big check for a cabin was another. There is always a wide gap between idea and implementation. It requires courage and conviction to jump across the chasm, to actually do something. *Is it worth it? Is rest so important? Am I doing the right thing? Am I a fool?* A decision must be made. Much is at stake. The safety of the abstract is gone. Yet without action, there is only good intentions. These are usually pursued by regret.

I bought the cabin.

The Plumbing Surprise

I bought the cabin in March. Since it was forty years old and had been neglected for a while, I knew that there were many things that needed tending. I had it inspected before I bought it, of course, but one area that could not be evaluated was the water system. Not to bore you with too many details, but the cabin has a cistern, a pump to get water out of the cistern, and the usual assortment of piping, fixtures, etc. At the time of the inspection the cabin was winterized, meaning that there was no water in the system and no way to check it out. However, I noticed that a few of the pipes were broken.

Later, when I explored more thoroughly under the cabin, I discovered that *most* of the pipes were broken. Yup, most. Now let me describe what it is like under the cabin. "Crawl space" is the term—not as in a hands-and-knees crawl but as in an on-your-belly-Marine Corps-under-machinegun-fire crawl. The floor was dirt—a very fine dusty kind of dirt. Above were floor joists upon which to bang my head. Got the picture?

I may have bought a cabin but I never seriously entertained the thought of hiring a plumber to do the repair job. I am still too cheap for that. If I could do something on my own, I would do it. Of course I did not know what I was doing, but I fancied that I could learn…and I did eventually. In the end I spent a considerable amount of time under the cabin. I figured that in the first few months of cabin ownership I spent more time under the cabin than in the cabin.

Is there some point here or are you just rambling on like old guys do?

So a question occurred to me under the cabin: Am I working or resting?

Work or Rest?

If you remember at the beginning of this book I defined rest as *not-work* Or, more completely, as *activities that refresh you after you have provided for the needs of yourself, your families and others.* Now, how would you answer the plumbing question? Work or rest? It is not so easy in real life, is it?

Since I had much time to ponder this in solitude under the cabin, let me step through my reasoning and share my conclusion. As always, you may not agree with me. I vacillated some myself.

Was the plumbing not-work? Well, on the one hand, I do not earn my bread as a plumber. It is clearly not my vocational work. It was a change from my vocational work. On the other hand, concerning providing for needs, plumbing provides for a very basic need. I need water. Without water the cabin would not be very useful for anything. So it is a split decision. It could go either way.

I then considered the aspect of refreshment. Did the plumbing refresh me from my work?

What kind of question is that? Are you crazy? You were crawling around trying to replace pipes! You were caked with dirt and sweat, bumps on your noggin, cramped in confined places! How could that possibly be refreshing?

Actually, I found the plumbing to be very refreshing. And not only the plumbing. I always have a job or two to do at the cabin—chop wood, replace boards in the deck, patch the roof. These are cabin activities that provide a break from my vocational work. They provide relief and distraction from the burdens I bear. Thus they are an excellent source of rest. If you could not view these type of jobs in the same light, if you would classify them as "additional work," I have some advice. Don't buy a cabin.

Don't buy a house either. A house provides many benefits. In addition to the obvious one, shelter, it is the primary place for nurturing our relationships—marriage, family and friendships. A house should become "home," a place of memories that we cherish, not merely a residence. I like houses and recommend that you get one. But, like a cabin, a house is a never ending project. There is always something that needs to be done. Some things, like plumbing or cutting the grass, require immediate attention, but others, like redecorating or remodeling, can be done at your leisure.

Before I wrote this book, I used to consider house projects to be work. I worked all day at the job and then come home and "worked" on the house at night. Weekends provided time for more "work" on the house. Work, work, work, work, work. No time for rest. Exhaustion.

I now classify these projects as rest. You may say that this is a distinction without a difference. *What difference does the label make?* The label makes a lot of difference if it accompanies a change of perspective. For me the difference is between working and resting when doing around-the-house jobs. Now I obtain rest in addition to accomplishing some beneficial tasks. This is the proverbial "killing two birds with one stone."

Useful Rest

You may be having trouble digesting the idea that cabin or house maintenance can be restful. The reason is that your concept of rest has been malformed. You simply do not associate productive endeavors with rest. Perhaps you were traumatized as a child when your parents told you to lie quietly on your bed and "rest" for a while. Association: rest equals not doing anything involving physical activity. Or perhaps, through ingrained habit, you only crave the amusement of the television, the computer or the gizmo when you are tired from work. Association: rest equals electronic immersion.

While these may have a limited place in your rest regimen, my point is that they should not be the only activities in your bucket. Why? Because they are generally the least effective forms of rest. They are like eating popcorn when you are trying to satisfy your hunger. You just keep eating and eating but end up only feeling bloated. You crave something more substantial. To get something more substantial, you must broaden your rest vocabulary to include more demanding—and more useful—pursuits.

Pursuits that provide the most refreshing rest are those that are most productive. These type of activities may create pleasant things like Churchill's paintings. Or they may produce useful things like Churchill's brickwork or my cabin plumbing. Rest activities may even put food on the table like fishing or hunting or gardening. Here are some productive rest ideas: cooking, furniture making, car maintenance or photography. This list is endless. Just because these activities may be vocational work for some does not mean that they are work for all. They may be good source of rest for you.

Nothing has been more helpful to me than understanding the nature of each thing I do. Is this activity work or rest? When this distinction is clearly in my mind, I work harder and rest better. When I have not formed a clear concept of what I am doing in a particular case, the purpose is muddled and I drift into uncertainty, wasting valuable time and opportunity. This is true for you too.

So know what you are doing. Put a mental label on every one of your activities. "This is work" or "This is rest." This is simple, yes?

Pesky Children and Disciples

Yes, the concept of labeling is fairly simple, but once again the actual practice of rest proves to be more difficult than theory.

People bring complications, especially the people you live with. They mess up your nicely compartmentalized categories. I remember when a hollow-eyed homeschooling mother once challenged me. She said, "My work is to raise my children. There is never a time when I am not raising them. Even if we are on vacation—or some other "rest" activity—I must instruct them on this or correct them on that. It NEVER stops! I NEVER get a break!"

Good point. I should mention that her husband was sitting beside her when she made this comment. Hopefully he picked up on her desperate plea. *Note to self: Give wife a night off so she doesn't crack up.*

A night off was surely deserved in this case, but it would not have resolved the larger question. The larger question is this: Is parenting unceasing work that permits no time for rest?

Let us again consider Jesus. He often ceased his public ministry and retreated to the desolate places to rest. He did not go alone. He took his disciples with him. They were always with him (except during those notable times when he prayed alone). That was the point of being a disciple—they were to be *with* him. So a question arises. Was discipling disciples work? If it was, Jesus was nearly always working because his disciples were nearly always with him. Could Jesus have said: "I NEVER get a break from working on those guys! I NEVER get any rest even when I retreat to the desolate places!"

I think not. There is an important distinction to make here. It is best to define discipleship as a *relationship* not as a work *activity*. In the discipling relationship Jesus was always teaching his disciples. He taught them during times of work and times of rest. He taught them *how* to work and rest. The teaching and other interaction that occurs in relationship should not be strictly classified as working.

As in discipleship, parenting never ceases. Parents are responsible to raise their children, to nurture and correct them. This is an unrelenting endeavor, as any parent will attest to. It is an endeavor that takes place in both work and rest activities. Often the lines between the two get blurred, especially in the cases of schooling or other teaching activities. But it will again help to carefully classify what is occurring.

I will once more pick on the homeschooling mom. When she is correcting Little Missy's algebra, she is working on her daughter's formal education. When she instructs Junior to eat his corn with his fork not his fingers, she is parenting during a meal, which is a rest activity. When on vacation, she should take a break from algebra but still insist on use of the silverware.

Parents should follow the example of Jesus with his disciples— using every teachable moment whether at work or rest—to raise their children. You can do this while resting together during a game or a mountain hike, as well as while working together during weeding the lawn or cooking dinner.

Church Time

In this chapter I have been defining what work is, what rest is and what is neither. These distinctions will help you understand the purpose of the things you do and, therefore, do them more effectively. Here is one more. Are you working or resting when you are engaged in church activities?

Hmmm. Hopefully you are thinking: *That depends.* Yes, it does. I'll start with the easiest role and climb up the ladder to the hardest.

You should agree that the pastor is working when he is preaching and teaching. Sunday is not a day of rest for him. It is a day of work, hard work. That is why the pastor usually takes Monday off. He needs to recover from his work. He needs to rest. No one carps about this— *I have to work on Monday. Why doesn't he?*—because even the dimmest among us grasps the obvious.

Climb a few rungs up the ladder. What about everyone else who serves or ministers on Sunday morning or at any other time of the week? This includes Sunday School teachers, nursery workers, youth leaders, committees, elder boards, counselors, musicians, women's and men's ministries, small group leaders, etc. Is this work too? Of course it is! All forms of ministry are work by definition. But for some reason, you look at these roles differently than you do for professional, i.e. paid, Christian workers. You create a third category of activities— "ministry," which you really do not consider to be either work or rest. This is a hot button issue for me, but since I will push the button in the next chapter, I will simply mention it here.

Now climb to the top of the ladder. Here is everyone who is not teaching, preaching, serving, leading, counseling or ministering in some way. What are they doing? Working or resting? I say that they are resting in this role. They are resting because they are not working. This in no way devalues their participation. There is great value in rest.

Church activities are a combination of work and rest. Every church member needs to minister to the body (work), as well as to be ministered to by the body (rest). You should both give and receive. Serve but also be renewed from your work through worship and learning and fellowship! This is how the body functions.

The Stupidest Idea Ever

One more thing.

You have a hardy laugh when you hear someone saying something really stupid, especially when they do not realize that it is stupid. The stupider the remark, the funnier it is. Trouble is, sometimes you do not laugh at nonsense when you hear it…because you do not know that it is ridiculous. Usually this is some axiom that you have heard again and again. Too bad. You miss the joke.

There is a very funny joke about work and rest. It goes something like this:

I love my job, so it is not really work to me.
or
He was one of those fortunate few whose work became his play.

There are two fallacies here. The first is that work is an inherently miserable undertaking and, therefore, enjoyable work cannot be work. The second is that if you enjoy your work, you will not need "play," meaning rest. In both cases, your attitude about work is the determining factor. The idea is that you can change the nature of work by how you feel about it.

But your feelings never change the nature of things. Work is not transformed into rest because you feel good about it. You should feel good about your work...most of the time at least. If you detest honest work then you have a problem, a sin problem. But regardless of your attitude, work is still work and you always require rest to recover from it.

Know What You Are Doing

This little chapter has been about correcting misconceptions about work and rest. Confusion muddles everything up. You won't know what you are doing or why you are doing it. Clear thinking and careful distinctions will improve both your work and rest. Determine the objective of each thing that you do.

CHAPTER SEVENTEEN

The Fellowship of the Exhausted

Why are Christians usually among the worst of resters? You should be the best of resters. But usually you are not. I have already mentioned some reasons for this regretful phenomenon—bad theology, unworkable "spirituality," and a misunderstanding of the dynamics of rest. Up till now I have focused mainly on the practice of rest in the spheres of employment and family. Now I am going to invade one more sphere—the sphere of Christian community, commonly referred to as "fellowship" or "church life."

It is here that you find collective support for your attempt to deny God's work-rest created order. You would more quickly tire of this impossible feat on your own, but through the encouragement of your brothers and sisters you persevere. To the New Testament "one another's," such as "love one another" and "encourage one another," you add "keep one another from resting."

Why this attitude is so prevalent in our churches? To understand it fully, I must separate those who get paid to minister from those who do not get paid.

Over Work for Professional Christians

First those that earn their bread by ministry. These are pastors, missionaries, counselors, para-church staff, etc. You pay them and rightly so. Supporting gifted workers allows them to devote more time to ministry and is the fulfillment of the biblical principle: "You shall not muzzle an ox when it treads out the grain," and, "The laborer deserves his wages" (1 Timothy 5:18). So far so good.

But many paid Christian workers seem compelled to over work and under rest. Furthermore, they seem compelled to tell everyone about it. Of course this is done subtly and in "spiritually correct" humility.

I must work longer than others to prepare a decent sermon, so it takes me thirty hours…on top of everything else.

Our people have so many deep problems that require counseling. I don't know how long I will be able to keep up with it all.

Those youth group kids keep me hopping day and night. No rest for the weary!

These type of statements injure both those who speak them and those who hear them. They injure those who speak them because of the sympathy and admiration they receive from those who hear them. When their behavior is rewarded, they provide more of it. These statements injure the hearers because they assume that they are to act the same way, i.e., work themselves to exhaustion.

But a thoughtful response would discourage this destructive behavior. Try this next time you hear someone dangling their over work in front of your nose in search of affirmation:

Missionary at a missions' conference:
There is no time to rest on the field. There is such a great need! I'm going to burn out rather than rust out. I'm all in for the Lord!

You, after you have finished this book:
I appreciate your enthusiasm, but burning yourself out is not a good stewardship of your time or of my money. Unless you start taking better care of yourself so that you can be more productive, I am going to have to withdraw my support.

Missionary (in shock):
But…but…I'll rest when I get to heaven.

You:
At this rate that will be sooner rather than later. Instead,
get the rest that you need. If you do, I'll keep the spigot on.

Perhaps this is a bit too harsh. But sometimes communication needs to be fresh and lively to be effective.

Why do those who make their living through ministry overwork? There are reasons. Perhaps it is an attempt to do the work of the entire Body of Christ instead of a more limited and targeted role as a specific member of the Body of Christ. Or it is an assumption that a "calling to the ministry" places this work on a higher level, transcending the rest needed for "worldly" work. Or it is an affection for romanticized biographies that imply that our heroes of the faith were all work and no play. Or it is cover for avoiding some particularly difficult area of ministry or for neglecting a spouse or children. Or, last but not least, it is behavior driven by insecurity—insecurity rooted in anxiety about not having a "real job."

Whatever the reason the result is the same. Exhausted workers harm themselves, their families and those that they serve because they lose their perspective, their enthusiasm, and their sense of humor. In other words, in their weariness they lose sight of the sovereign Lord Jesus and their particular role in his kingdom. Their yoke is hard and their burden is heavy.

Now wait just one minute! You are criticizing the most dedicated among us!

What I am criticizing is the neglect of rest and the resulting exhaustion. Hard work is commendable. You should exemplify diligent, consistent, productive hard work in every area of responsibility. However, pushing yourselves to the point that you can no longer work well is foolishness. You need to discern the difference between the two. You also need to develop the discipline to *stop* working and rest after you have labored in ministry.

While you are reeling from that, let me throw another punch.

Under Rest for the Volunteers

It is not only paid ministers that have the well-intentioned but destructive problem of over working. So do those who labor in ministry for free. Although many of the causes and impacts are the same for both groups, the laity (for lack of a better term) have a complicating factor. You do not usually count your ministry as work.

You may be skeptical of this point. If so, answer this question: "How many hours did you work this week?" The instinctive response, usually, is to count only the hours spent in your bread-earning vocation. So let us see how this plays out. If you are a doctor and spent sixty hours this week practicing medicine and six hours preparing for and teaching a Sunday school class, you would usually respond that have worked sixty hours. But the preacher who spent six hours preparing for and teaching a Sunday school class would add that time to his 40 hours of other ministry-related work and respond that he has worked forty-six hours. Is the work of teaching only work for the one who is paid to do it? No, of course not. The work is the same for both and so is the need to rest, to recuperate from the work. This is true for all ministry—counseling, evangelizing, serving, leading, etc.

For some the malady is even worse. These earnest saints think that ministry is the means that God provides to refresh them from all of their other work—their "secular" work. As I covered the source of this disease in the first part of this book, I will only address the glaring disconnect here. Does more work refresh you from work? Does work in one sphere restore you from work in another sphere? No, it does not.

Wait! I've got you now! You keep blathering on about how rest involves the elements of change and concentration. Doesn't ministry involve both? It is a change from my other work and certainly requires my concentration. Why can't I consider it to be rest?

Because the Bible calls it work. There is great wisdom here, of course. All work requires a following rest. You cannot cheat this reality because your work takes different forms. After one form of work you must find a form of rest that provides a change from that particular work. Even if your day job is substantially different than our ministry work, you need the appropriate rest from both exertions.

Through Your Eyes

There is another reason why you overwork and under rest in Christian community, and this one is not affected by whether or not you are paid for ministry work. It the perspective you have because of your spiritual gifts. This gifting forms a lens through which you view the needs around you. It determines which ones you consider to be the most critical and urgent.

On the one hand, a teacher is obsessed with the need to understand the Bible. For this saint, every weakness or strength in the church is traceable to a theological root. On the other hand, a server looks around and sees the need to clean up the kitchen or take a meal to the stricken. Is one perspective superior? No, of course not. A properly functioning church requires teachers *and* kitchen cleaners. The member who recognizes a need should offer his service to meet the need. The teacher should teach. The server should serve. Both should do so cheerfully, remembering that ultimately they are serving the Lord.

But a problem begins to grow when you over work and become weary. You wonder why you are not getting more help. You assume it is because "those people" are not doing their part. Tensions soon arise.

Where is everyone else around here?

Why am I always the one who has to clean the kitchen?

Nobody else volunteers to teach this Sunday school class!

I never get a break because nobody else will do the work!

But you do not see what everyone else is doing. The Lord does, but you do not. And, by the way, what everyone else is doing goes beyond the walls of the church building and the confines of ministry programs. You sometimes forget this because you have neglected rest and made yourself vulnerable to all sorts of temptations.

Be content to serve in the area of your giftedness, but at the same time guard against overwork and its accompanying sins of complaining, bitterness and division. If you need rest from ministry work, you should take it. If you think that God's universe will grind to a halt without you turning the crank or that his eternal purposes will be frustrated, then perhaps you think too highly of yourself. So rest. And when you are rested, you will again be able to work heartily in your niche.

Friendly Fire

Having said this, I realize that not everyone is working in ministry, doing their part. There really are some slackers, loafers, dead beats, pew warmers. *I know who those people are! They don't do anything!* Yes, sadly so. They stick out like sore thumbs. Every time you think of some understaffed ministry, you think of those slugs who do nothing.

No one is more aware of this than the pastor. On Sunday morning he peers over the pulpit and sees them. There they are—starting to doze off, texting someone, looking bored. He is not just thinking about them now. He has been thinking about them all week during his sermon preparation. At every point of application he has them in mind. So he has meticulously prepared his rhetorical arrows that will pierce their hard hearts. And now, at long last, he lets them fly.

> *Awake, sleeper! Put your back into the harvest! Every hand is needed on deck! There is no "I" in "team." The time is short! The reward is great! Every moment must be redeemed for the kingdom! Quit wasting your life!*

But an odd thing happens. Actually, it is not odd because it happens the same way every Sunday. The sharp, deadly arrows of application fly straight and true, aimed at the Chief of Slackers Harry Slugmump...and pass right through him with no effect. But they keep going and hit the most exhausted saint in the congregation, dear Henrietta Tenderheart.

> *Oh my! I have been wasting too much time. I read that book I so enjoyed. Six hours lost for eternity! I must serve in the nursery more. And I will spend every evening going door-to-door collecting used tea bags for our overseas missionaries.*

Harry is an idler, of course. He is neglecting his ministry work. Henrietta is certainly no idler but makes the opposite error of over work. Harry never gets on the horse. Henrietta continuously falls off of it. Neither of them displays the balance of the work-rest created order.

Henrietta would be receptive to good biblical teaching concerning rest, but she never hears it. Why? Because most preachers are fixated on Harry. They fear that teaching about the blessings of rest would encourage the Harrys to continue in their idleness. But this only proves that they fail to distinguish between rest, which is a reward for work, and idleness, which is the avoidance of work.

Worse yet, by neglecting rest teaching, preachers withhold truth that would be a great blessing to the Henriettas and, as a result, to the church as a whole. Instead the poor Henriettas absorb the continuous exhortations to *work-work-work* directed at the Harrys, who are comfortably ignoring the preacher anyway. Perhaps it is time to consider the needs of those who hear.

Sabbaticals

Nothing reveals the dysfunctional environment concerning rest in Christian community as does sabbaticals. The purpose of a sabbatical is to provide a period of time—usually a couple of months—for a worker to step away from the burdens of ministry work in order to recuperate and become refreshed. In other words, sabbaticals are for rest, substantial rest. Great concept, but we manage to mess it up.

I will again separate the sheep from the goats, the paid from the unpaid, because each group approaches sabbaticals differently.

Regarding the paid, many churches schedule sabbaticals for their pastors every so many years, as do many para-church ministries for their workers. This is wisdom. However, the actual practice of sabbatical often lessens its restorative value. How so? By loading up this time of rest with work.

I have a dream that someday we will say something like this to our paid workers:

> *We are giving you three months to step aside from your ministry work. The purpose is to provide you with a long, deep rest. This rest is essential to you, your family and the ministry at large. Do not waste this opportunity. We cannot afford such foolishness and neither can you. We trust you to use this time wisely by doing the things that will truly refresh you. You know what these are. We do not. Now get out of here. When you return, those bags under your eyes had better be gone, as well as that surly disposition you have been nurturing.*

Unfortunately my dream is unrealized. Instead of the above, we give instructions something along the lines of this:

> *We are giving you a three-month sabbatical, but you had better not goof off. Just to be sure, we have a few requirements. First, you will read through this list of two dozen ministry-related books. Second, you will thoroughly evaluate the philosophy and practice of our ministry and prepare at least three ground-breaking, revolutionary recommendations. Third, you will complete your doctorate degree. Fourth, you will write a book that will become a best seller. Fifth, you will report on your progress every two weeks, with a comprehensive briefing upon your return. Good luck. May God be with you.*

Amazingly, even though sabbaticals are more like the latter than the former, they still provide some rest benefit for paid workers. This cannot be said for the unpaid.

You've Been Left Behind

Why do unpaid Christian workers, i.e. the laity, not benefit from sabbaticals? Because you do not get sabbaticals. Why do you not get sabbaticals? For the same reason mentioned above—because you do not really consider ministry work to be work in the same sense that those who are paid to do it. Of course work is work. And work requires rest. This reality is not altered by your misconceptions.

But you may say that because you are not doing this work "full time," you do not require rest from this work. To which I would reply that rest is a ceasing of labor at whatever frequency that labor occurs. It is a pause in the rhythm of work. Take Sunday school teaching, for instance. This work occurs at a once-a-week rhythm—preparation during the week and teaching on Sunday morning. Note that this is the same exact rhythm as preaching. But somehow you think the Sunday school teacher gets the rest he needs during the week, while you know that the preacher needs pulpit relief after so many Sundays plus a longer sabbatical now and then. So the paid get a break while the unpaid labor on endlessly, week after week.

What is the result? It is never good. I have already mentioned the complaining, bitterness and division that takes place within a church or organization. Sometimes—far too frequently—the overworked and under rested will leave altogether. The reasons are never clear and even less satisfying.

I can't explain it, but I sense God's call to another church.

I need to find others of kindred spirit.

I am just worn down here.

So they seek a new place and new faces when all they really need is rest.

Here is the conclusion of the matter: Sabbaticals for everyone who works, both the paid and unpaid.

Leading From the Front

Leadership is responsible for the care of members in a church or organization. This includes ensuring that the structures of their ministries accommodate the work-rest created order. Leaders must begin with themselves, not modeling workaholism but hard work followed by refreshing rest.

Let the Church rest. She will be healthier and more attractive.

CHAPTER EIGHTEEN

Idleness Revisited

First a short review of the relationship between rest and work.

The one (rest) is the negative of the other (work). That is, rest is not-work. Yet rest and work are inseparable. They form a pair that are always together, like peanut butter and jelly or faith and works. There is also an unalterable order between the two—rest follows work and work precedes rest. You cannot rest prior to work, only after it. Rest is the caboose not the engine. You rest *from* work not *for* work. However, after you have successfully completed a work-rest cycle, you are ready to begin again and work with vigor. Finally, there is a paradox. While rest consumes time that could be used for work, decreasing rest decreases work and increasing rest increases work. These are the interactions between rest and work, but they all begin with what rest is not.

There is one more thing that rest is not. Rest is not idleness. Unfortunately, many people—perhaps most...perhaps you—think that they are the very same thing. You think that any activity other than work must be idleness. This wraps you in a fog of confusion about living a full, complete life to the glory of God. How do you find a way out of this fog?

Clarity is needed. The fog must lift. For this I will revisit what the Bible says about idleness.

The Slugfest

Here is the most extensive passage concerning idleness.

Now we command you, brothers, in the name of our Lord Jesus Christ, that you keep away from any brother who is walking in **idleness** and not in accord with the tradition that you received from us. For you yourselves know how you ought to imitate us, because we were not **idle** when we were with you, nor did we eat anyone's bread without paying for it, but with toil and labor we worked night and day, that we might not be a burden to any of you. It was not because we do not have that right, but to give you in ourselves an example to imitate. For even when we were with you, we would give you this command: If anyone is not willing to work, let him not eat. For we hear that some among you walk in **idleness**, not busy at work, but busybodies. Now such persons we command and encourage in the Lord Jesus Christ to do their work quietly and to earn their own living.

II Thessalonians 3:6-12

Let me draw a definition from this. Idleness is not working. That is, the idler is "not willing to work." He has the ability to work but chooses not to. There is work to be done, but he refuses to do it.

The Apostle Paul contrasts this behavior with his own. Paul worked hard at tent making to earn his own bread although he had every right to be supported by his ministry work (see I Corinthians 9:4-6). This is really an extraordinary endorsement of the importance of work! It is also reveals the length the apostle would go to guard the church against idleness. His exhortation is needed as much in our day as it was in his. No, perhaps the warning against idleness is needed more in our day since the welfare state blunts the consequence of idleness, i.e. hunger. But welfare state or no, in these cases the church is to exercise discipline. "...keep away from any brother who is walking in idleness."

I will move on to the Proverbs.

The sluggard does not plow in the autumn;
he will seek at harvest and have nothing.
Proverbs 20:12

The desire of the sluggard kills him,
for his hands refuse to labor.
Proverbs 21:25

The sluggard says, "There is a lion outside!
I shall be killed in the streets!"
Proverbs 22:13

As a door turns on its hinges,
so does a sluggard on his bed.
Proverbs 26:14

Christians love to quote these proverbs, especially the last two as they are fine satire. But there is nothing funny about the lesson. Poverty and death are the end for those who refuse to work. Idleness is as serious a sin in the Old Testament as it is in the New.

You sometimes think of these verses when you see a healthy young bum snoozing on a park bench, which is a correct application, but you more often incorrectly apply them to yourself when you are resting. Because you do not properly distinguish rest from idleness, you assume that you are sinning when you are resting. And the resulting guilt—deserved or not—always decreases the quality of your rest.

At the beginning of this chapter I described the relationship between rest and work. Now I will describe the relationship between idleness and work.

I was wondering that myself.

Good. You're still awake.

Idleness and work are never together. This is because idleness eliminates work. Work has the same effect on idleness. One kills the other. They cannot coexist. Idleness corrupts, distorts and aborts the work-rest created order. Ultimately, idleness is a lie. It is a lie about God that is told every time a person is idle. Why? Because man was made to reflect the image of God. And God is no idler.

Because idleness eliminates work, it also eliminates rest. You can only rest after you have worked, just as you only get dessert after you have finished your supper. If you do not work, you cannot rest. The idler thinks that he can cheat the system and obtain the blessing of rest, but he does not. You cannot be refreshed from work unless you have first worked.

The Satiation Nation

Therefore, the idler finds that his idleness is less satisfying than anticipated. His solution? More idleness. He reasons that the problem must be that he is not getting enough. So he doubles down on his idleness, like the drunk drinks or the glutton eats.

> The sluggard buries his hand in the dish
> and will not even bring it back to his mouth.
> Proverbs 19:24

But more idleness never satisfies. Excess satiates. Instead of fulfillment the idler purchases boredom. He becomes dull, self-centered, apathetic, jaded, pitiful, ridiculous. If he has any self-awareness, which he seldom does, he will loath himself. If he does not, others will do it for him. Work is the simple antidote, but the idler despises that above all.

Let's Talk About Me

At this point, friend, I'll bet that you are thinking about some idlers that you know.

Yup, that describes _____ perfectly. He is really in trouble!

He probably is. But this is not about him. This is about you.

You probably are not a person who refuses to earn his bread. You work for a living. But an aggravating and consistent theme of Jesus' teaching was that he will judge not only your public persona and deeds but also your inward motivations and hidden actions. You still manage to waste some time in idleness, don't you? You are clever enough not to display your idleness in public, like the staggering drunk downtown. You are much more discreet.

But you said earlier that I incorrectly condemn myself for idleness. Am I guilty or not? Make up your mind!

I said that you often think that you are committing the sin of idleness when you are in fact resting. You should not feel guilty for resting, but you should for idleness. The trick is to discern the difference between the two. Admittedly, this is not simple. You need to figure out where the lines are for you. Let each one be convinced in his own mind so that he may serve God with a clear conscience.

The difficulty in distinguishing idleness from rest is that most activities can be either. Just as various activities can be work or rest in a given situation, so it is with idleness and rest. One man's rest may be the other's idleness. This is true for every activity I describe in the next section. For example, one may read books to rest from work. Another may read books to evade work. In the first case the reading is rest. In the second it is idleness. You should ask yourself: *What is the purpose of this activity? Is it recovery from work or avoidance of work?* This simple question will reveal the nature of an activity.

What About Those Gizmos?

Take another look at your electronic gizmos. My criticism earlier was that they form a habit of mind that is detrimental to concentration and, therefore, to rest. Now I will pick at them from the angle of idleness.

Get over it you…you Luddite! Welcome to the 21ˢᵗ Century. Gizmos are here to stay.

All the more reason to critique them. Gizmos are a powerful temptation to idleness. In the first place, they provide *ready access* to a variety of activities that may be used for idleness—games, internet surfing, email, news, etc. It is one thing to resist a temptation that requires some effort to obtain. It is quite another when the temptation is right there in your pocket or purse or sitting on your desk. In the second place, gizmos provide *private access*. Only you can see what is on that little screen. Nobody else knows what you are looking at. During the sermon your dad may assume that you are reading the biblical passage and diligently taking notes, when in fact you are texting Joey to check out the new girl in pew five. Or your boss may think you are reviewing information pertaining to the meeting, when actually you are looking for a good deal on shoes.

Add ready and private access to the mentally addictive nature of gizmos and you have a super machine that is ready to make an idler out of you. All you have to do is cooperate and – kazam! – you have turned into a slug.

But…but…ah….

Do not attempt to explain. I can do it for you. *It relaxes me. It is how I stay in touch. I will miss out if I don't keep up. Nearly everyone is doing it.* Okay. That last one is certainly undeniable. Nearly everyone else is doing it. Fifteen minutes of observation in any public place will prove this. I recently sat next to a young lady on a cross-country flight. She never spoke or looked around. For the entire flight (minus the restrictions during take-off and landing) she peered into her little gizmo screen. Since I was sitting next to her, I stole a glance now and then. A game.

Maybe she was resting!

Maybe she was. Regardless, I am only pointing out that people are spending a whole lot of time on their gizmos. Maybe you are. If so, you should evaluate how you are using it and for what purpose. And, even if you do find some gizmo activities to be restful, I hope to persuade you that there are much better ways to obtain rest.

Porn-A-Potty

Gizmos are useful for work and *may* be useful at times for rest, but there is one gizmo activity that has absolutely no redeeming value. Pornography. It is ugly, corrupting, consuming, enslaving. Pornography used to be almost exclusively a male sin, but it is now an increasingly female sin. It is rampant—not just in the culture at large, but among us Christians. Unfortunately gizmos (and all its electronic cousins) are an enabling technology. That is because gizmos provide ready and private access to pornography just as they do for everything else.

Pornography is mental fornication. It deadens the soul. It steals your life. It drains a marriage. It saps the motivation to marry. It shames you before God and man. It does all of these nasty things. But I will dwell no further on these consequences. My purpose is to correctly categorizing the activity. How do you classify pornography? Is it work or rest or idleness?

Work first. Can pornography be work? Well, it is work for the pornographer. An occupation need not be God-honoring to qualify as work. Work is simply the activity by which one earns a living, regardless of its morality. But the question here is not the production of pornography but the partaking of it. With this qualification, pornography cannot be work. Lusting does not put bread on the table.

What about rest? A rest activity may also be either moral or immoral, so pornography is not automatically disqualified because it is sinful. People engage in many sinful activities in order to obtain rest—drunkenness, drug abuse, gambling, to name a few others. If these things follow work, they must be classified as rest. The practitioner is seeking refreshment from his work. Of course these activities do not provide very effective rest. Picture a teenager retching at a drinking party or a hollowed-eyed porn addict staying up to the wee hours of the morning. Satisfying rest? Hardly. But just as lousy work is still work, so it is with rest.

Finally, is pornography idleness? Yes, if it consumes the time you should be working. You usually think of idleness in the sense of never getting to your work. But idleness also occurs when you extend your rest activities beyond the time needed to refresh yourself. You need to conclude your rest and get back to work. While it is true that addictive behavior, such as pornography, is much more likely to become idleness, any rest activity—even the good ones—may become a vehicle for you to avoid work if you prolong them.

But, just to be clear, you should never indulge in the sin of pornography.

Well, enough of this wretched topic.

Kick The Bucket

To sum up, you should work hard, rest well and avoid idleness. Regrettably you cannot do this by accident. You must *know* what you are doing. If you do not have a clear understanding of these terms, you may confuse your rest with idleness and your idleness with rest. In both cases you are not being a good steward. You are not redeeming the time.

So faithful living begins with a good vocabulary.

> Work: Activities that provide for needs.
> Rest: Activities that refresh from work.
> Idleness: Activities that avoid work.

Just knowing these definitions is not enough, of course. You must apply them. You must stick one of these labels on each of your activities. This requires wisdom and persistence. Wisdom to discern the nature of an activity. Persistence to continually evaluate to what end you are using it in a particular instance.

Return to the bucket metaphor. I described two buckets earlier—work and rest. Idleness is the third and final bucket. Everything you do goes into one of these buckets. You are always filling one bucket at any one time. With one hand you hold the bucket and with the other you fill it. It is impossible to fill two or three buckets at once. It is also impossible not to fill any bucket. There is no dead time. You are always doing something.

Work　　　**Rest**　　　**Idleness**

Always strive to be filling either the work bucket or the rest bucket with Christ-honoring activities. And every time you are tempted to idleness, kick away that bucket and pick up one of the others. To do this, you will need much more than good intentions. You will need good structure.

CHAPTER NINETEEN

Structure

Whether you admit it or not, you are a creature of habit.

You cut a furrow for every aspect of your life and then follow it again the next time you bring the plow around. Why? Because it is the easiest thing to do. Most of what happens in life is predictable and repeatable—your work, your rest, and your idleness. You do not constantly invent new and creative ways to tie your shoes, drive to work, prepare breakfast, get the kids ready to go, shop, exercise, check the gizmo, watch TV or sleep. For the most part, you do these things the way you did them the time before…and the time before that, etc. You repeat learned patterns for things both small and large.

My interest is not in the multitude of your quirky little habits, like whether you squeeze the toothpaste tube from the end or in the middle. My interest is in your substantial habits—the ones that significantly shape how you spend your time. I call these habits "structure." Simply then, structure is your recurring activity habits.

Maria and the Captain

Everyone has structure. In this sense, everyone is "structured." But perhaps you object.

I'm not structured! I'm not stuck in a rut! I'm a creative, free-spirited person.
or
I am really undisciplined. I have little structure in my life. I need more of it.

Is that so? Consider the main characters from *The Sound of Music*. There is Maria the aspiring nun and new governess for the von Trapp children. And there is Captain von Trapp their father. There could not be two more different people. The Captain is a rigid disciplinarian. Maria is the freest of free-spirits. The Captain blows his whistle so that his children respond with military precision. Maria dresses the children in curtains and they romp all over Salzburg, Austria, singing movie hits. This leads to tension followed by marriage, as dictated by our expectations for romance…but I digress.

The question is: Does the Captain live a structured life and Maria live an unstructured one? No. They both live structured lives. The structures are just very different. The Captain's structure—supposedly—is attributable to his military background, which instilled a habit of regimented order for every task. Maria's habits, on the other hand, do not conform to regimented order. This much is obvious, but do not assume that Maria is completely spontaneous, always plowing a new furrow in new ground. No she doesn't. Her habits and structures are as predictable as the Captain's. Her ingrained patterns of living express themselves in the von Trapp household in the same way they expressed themselves at the abbey. Even Hollywood gets basic structure theory right.

Enough of movie characters. The point is that you must not confuse *style* of structure with the *fact* of structure. One who is habitually late to meetings is just as structured as one who is habitually early. One who repeatedly plops in front of the television in a persistently vegetative state is as structured as one who regularly reads good, enriching books. Everyone has structure.

There is another aspect about structure that is universal. You *choose* it. Now I know that it is popular to attribute your actions to personality type or economic class or ethnic background or age or career or something else. While these things certainly influence you, they do not remove your personal responsibility to order your life in a way that brings glory to God. Even if you are forced into an undesirable structure, such as Joseph was in his enslavement and imprisonment in Egypt, you are still accountable for what you do.

So be wise with your structure, carefully building good activity habits for work and rest, replacing bad ones, and eliminating idleness. As the old saying goes, you form your habits and your habits form you.

Structure Structure

In addition to the elements of habit and choice, structure involves the element of time. You experience time primarily in days, weeks and years.

Each of these has its own natural cycle or rhythm. The most fundamental daily rhythms involve sleeping and eating. You fit all of your work, rest and idleness into the time that remains. The time that remains is largely structured by weeks and years. Weeks are divided by work hours, transportation, household duties, church activities, sports, clubs, shopping, etc. For most, weekends provide a different agenda and rhythm than work weeks. Years provide the final overlay, adding structure that includes holidays, vacations, birthdays, anniversaries, and other annually recurring events.

You may have a job that completely messes up these traditional time structures. Perhaps you are a mother with an infant, a nurse, a Marine, a small business owner, a pastor, or must travel a lot. If so, you do not have a banker's rhythm—a regular eight-to-five workweek with weekends and holidays off. Nope, that is not your structure. But you still have a structure. It is just a different structure.

I know of what I speak. For two years I worked a rotating schedule that consisted of four swing shifts followed by four graveyard shifts followed by four day shifts followed by three days off. This seriously disrupted all three of the natural time rhythms. I am thankful that I experienced this in my youth when I was more resilient. I do not think any permanent emotional damage was done, but there is no question that this was a challenging stretch for me. Nevertheless, it was no excuse for me to lapse into idleness. No, I still had stewardship responsibility and accountability. In order to faithfully fulfill these, I strived to purposely build Christ-honoring work and rest structures within the time framework I found myself. And, whatever your situation, so should you.

So think structurally. Ask yourself questions like these: *How can I form daily, weekly and yearly routines that will help me work hard, rest well and avoid idleness? How can dinner time be transformed from a quick "pit stop" in front of the television to the focal point of family conversation? What traditions should I establish for Christmas? When is the best time each day for Bible reading and prayer? How can I consistently read good books? Where should I exercise regularly and how will this fit into my weekly schedule?*

Change Points

Another aspect of structure is that it will change. In addition to daily variability, every stage of life comes pre-packaged in structure— different structure. These are the "seasons of life." From childhood through old age, every season brings with it a unique structural framework. This may be schooling or jobs or family or ailments. Each one will significantly determine how you spend our time.

The bottom line is that you move through life passing from one structure to another. Even if you are settled comfortably into your current structure, circumstances will change and you will need to make adjustments before you know it. You have no choice in the matter. If you are in school, you may graduate...hopefully...someday. If you are single, you may get married. If you are married, you may lose your spouse. You may be blessed with children, but they will grow up and eventually leave. They may start their own families, which will draw upon your time in new ways. If you have a job, you may be fired or voluntarily leave it for a better one. Life is in motion and the motion causes structural adjustment. The more significant the life change, the more your structure is impacted.

I call the transition involved in structural alteration a "change point." A change point occurs when you stop doing one habitual activity and start doing another. Sometimes change points, like those above, are created externally by circumstances. But you may also create your own change points internally. That is, you may choose to adjust your structure because you want a better one. Perhaps you have a sinful habit and, by God's grace, you are compelled to end it. Or you are motivated, not by the negative but by the positive. You want to trade up, that is, to improve your structure from good to better or from better to best. You desire to make the most of every opportunity, to number your days, to be careful how you live, to seize the moment.

Whether externally or internally driven, there is a process that occurs in a change point.

Putting Off – Putting On

In the Unconcentrating chapter I introduced the "replacement" principle. I claim no credit for the concept because it is blatantly repeated throughout New Testament. You are commanded time and again to *put off* the old and *put on* the new. The "new" is to reflect the glorious truth of what Christians *are* in the risen Christ. The old is to be set aside because it reeks of what you *were* in fallen Adam. Or, to put it another way, you must act consistently with the spiritual reality of your salvation. Prove your faith. Show your love. Live true. Persevere.

Structural change always involves this concept of putting off and putting on. These are the two halves of the one whole. You cannot put off *or* put on. You must put off *and* put on. Why? Think about it. If you want to stop an activity, you simply cannot eliminate the time slot that it fills. Time will tick along and you must do something during that time. What will it be? Unless it is replaced, it will be the old activity that you are trying to get rid of because it is ingrained in your routine through habit. The old activity is the automatic default option. It is the furrow that your plow naturally follows. Conversely, you cannot establish a new activity until you have a time opening for it. You cannot put a peg in a hole until there is a hole available.

Let me flesh out this concept. Say that you desire two changes to your structure. One is negative (remove) and the other is positive (add). The negative is to stop watching so much television. The positive is to start exercising more. Now for some details. You watch the TV news from 5:30 to 6:00 p.m. every weekday evening before dinner. After reading this chapter you realize that this is not the best structural use of your time. So you decide to stop watching the news. Very noble.

But what happens tomorrow at 5:30? You have just driven home from work and the next recurring activity is dinner at 6:00. You are determined not to watch the news, but what are you going to do? You are bored. You sit down in the living room like you always do. There is the television remote. You look at it. You pick it up. You wonder what is happening in the world and if the weather will change. You hesitate. You resist. But…if you wait any longer, you are going to miss the headlines! *Click.*

On the positive side of structural change you desire to add more exercise. Very noble. Good intentions. The problem is when. Your structure—like all other structures—is largely filled up. *But wait! Ah, there is an opening this week on Thursday at 8 p.m. Eureka!* Due to your iron determination and strength of will you even follow through and go to the gym on Thursday night. Congratulations. Although you had hoped to exercise every night, at least this is a start. Now for week two.

Hmmm. That Thursday 8 p.m. slot is taken by the monthly Needlepoint Crafters Society meeting. How about eating dinner late on Tuesday? No, everyone will get cranky and Junior has his science fair project due on Wednesday. How about getting up at 5 a.m.? No, I need more than six hours of sleep. How about…. It is only too predictable how this will end: lots of frustration with a little guilt sprinkled on top.

What to do? So far you have failed to cut down your television time and to increase your exercise time. The solution begins with thinking structurally.

Okay, I can get this. What if…I…use that 5:30 to 6:00 p.m. slot to exercise? Now you are catching on.

I can walk for half an hour right after I get home. I won't turn on the TV. I'll put my exercise shoes on right away and head to the park. Good. *The time is there. I'm replacing one activity with another. This will work! I can do this!*

Tough Love for Widows

This simple example illustrates the basic dynamic of structural change, but most real-life circumstances are a bit more complex. The Apostle Paul gives us one. His context concerns church financial support for widows.

> Let a widow be enrolled if she is not less than sixty years of age, having been the wife of one husband, and having a reputation for good works: if she has brought up children, has shown hospitality, has washed the feet of the saints, has cared for the afflicted, and has devoted herself to every good work. But refuse to enroll younger widows, for when their passions draw them away from Christ, they desire to marry and so incur condemnation for having abandoned their former faith. Besides that, they learn to be idlers, going about from house to house, and not only idlers, but also gossips and busybodies, saying what they should not. So I would have younger widows marry, bear children, manage their households, and give the adversary no occasion for slander.
>
> I Timothy 5:9-14

Now I will freely—very freely—paraphrase this passage using my structure terminology.

Here are guidelines for supporting widows. The loss of a
husband is one of the most difficult change points
imaginable, but the church must be very careful to do what
is best structurally for a woman. If the woman is over sixty
years of age, has been faithful and has an established
history of good works, by all means provide for her
financially. This will enable her to continue to devote her
time to serving the saints and building up the church. She
is well suited for this structure. However, do not
permanently support younger widows. I know that you
may think that this would be the compassionate and loving
thing but it is not. Here is why. In her grief the woman is
vulnerable to making commitments that she may not keep.
She may feel that she will be completely dedicated to the
ministries of the church and her only work will be to serve
the saints. However, after a time she may desire to marry
again and have children. This is a natural human yearning
and not "unspiritual" in any way. But if before God and
church she has foolishly vowed to remain single and then
re-marries, she will violate her commitment and her
conscience. Think about the structural aspects of this
situation. If the young widow is supported, her work will
be going from house to house in order to "serve" others.
But instead of focusing on their interests, her repressed
desire to marry will lead to gossip and busybodyness. In
other words, your good intentions to provide for her will
actually enable her idleness! It will be much better if she
re-marries and fills her time with the Christ-honoring
structure of being a committed wife and mother. This will
thwart the devil's scheme to trap some in celibacy for
which they are not suited and to attack the church for the
resulting mischief.

Construction Zone

The final aspect of structure concerns transition time. How long does
it take to make a structural change? It depends. When a change point
is created by external circumstances, such as illustrated in widowhood
above, structure must change. There is no transitional period needed
to "lock in" a new habit and "lock out" an old one. Old structure has
been eliminated by new circumstances. The inevitable consequence is

that new structure will fill in the empty time slot. There is a question of *what* the new structure will be but not *if* the change will occur.

However for a change point that you initiate in order to improve your structure—such as devotional time, exercise, reading, etc.—the rule of thumb is that it takes about three weeks. That is, if you faithfully practice the new activity for three weeks, you will have established a new habit. You must be persistent and disciplined. But after a time the power of habit will work for you instead of against you.

You may also enlist the support of others to make structural improvements. This may be a close friend who will hold you accountable for your actions. Or it may be an institution, such as a school, a club or a team, which will impose regularly scheduled activities for you. In any case, the expectations of others are a very powerful influence in shaping structure. Of course, the influence may be bad (gang membership) or good (the community dodge ball league). For Christians, the local church should be the most significant influence, both at the personal and institutional levels. The activities of the church and the associated fellowship are a primary means God provides for good structure building.

For those enslaved by sinful private habits, do not think that you can re-structure on your own. You have been on your own, which is why you are in this mess. Humble yourself. Seek and accept the help of others. The body of Christ is to build one another up. You need them to build good structure in your life. And, by the way, they need you too.

Getting To The Cabin

Let's move along. You have dwelt on my private sins long enough. Besides, I thought this book was supposed to be about cabins…or rest. You haven't mentioned either one lately. You just keep chattering on and on about habits or structure or whatever! When are you getting to the meat and potatoes?

Persevere, dear reader. This excursion in structure was absolutely necessary. The next section will get down to the "meat and potatoes," as you say. In fact, I will weave together all the practical aspects of rest—change, concentration and structure—in application. And I will have something more to say about cabins.

But first I have a few more chapters on rest theory.

CHAPTER TWENTY

The Rest-O-Meter

Since you have been thinking about structure—the ordering of your life—a question naturally arises. What is the ratio between work and rest? Or, less mathematically and more simply, how long should you rest?

The Divine Ratio

At first glance, the Bible seems to provide a forthright answer to this question when God's rest is described:

> And on the seventh day God finished his work that he had done, and he rested on the seventh day from all his work that he had done.
>
> Genesis 2:2

...and then the pattern is applied to man:

> Six days you shall labor, and do all your work, but the seventh day is a Sabbath to the LORD your God.
>
> Exodus 20:9-10

So then, the ratio must be six to one. Six of work and one of rest. Right?

That seems right, but I know that you are up to your trickery! So why don't you just charge ahead into one of your convoluted explanations of why there isn't a straightforward answer to this question.

Okay. I'll begin with the six days of work. What does *six days* mean in relation to God? Does God experience time as we do? Is it sequential for him? Is he *outside* of time? Is there another dimension? I don't know, and I am not going speculate. This seems to be an exercise of the pot attempting to explain the nature of the potter, to put a twist on a biblical metaphor. I am content to humbly accept what God has revealed about himself and not attempt to fill in the blanks to my own satisfaction.

But I have some experience with how humans experience time. You experience it in twenty-four hour days. Given this, you do not work six entire days—144 hours. It would kill you. In fact you do not usually work through one entire day. Only under extraordinary circumstances would you work through a day or two. And if you did, you would soon collapse from exhaustion. Working entire days is not sustainable.

Beddy Bye Time

You may quibble and say that a twenty-four hour day encompasses the time for sleep. *Sleeping is downtime. It is off-the-clock. It is not a part of the work-rest formula.* The problem with this argument is that sleeping is rest. Sleeping is not doing nothing. It is a rest activity. This is so commonly understood that the phrase "get some rest" usually means "get some sleep." Sleep is the most fundamental and important rest. You need it every day. If you are not getting the sleep you require, there is no sense in concerning yourself with other rest activities…or work activities, for that matter. You must first have sleep rest.

How much sleep do you need? If you are an average person, you require around eight hours of sleep a day to be fully restored by sleep. Now apply the six-to-one ratio to determine how long you must work in order to earn that eight hours of sleep. You would need to work six hours for one hour of sleep and forty-eight hours for eight hours of sleep.

6 X 8 Sleep Hours = 48 Work Hours

Hmmm. There is an immediate problem here. It will take you two entire twenty-four hour days to earn one night's sleep.

The Rest of Rest

But the difficulty is worse than that. Conceding the point that your physical frailty requires you to sleep eight hours a day, what about the other sixteen? Do you work these sixteen hours straight through? No, you don't. You rarely, if ever, work sixteen hours straight without a break. What you do—by necessity—is take some rest while "working." This may be a stretching of the legs at the office, a chat about the Final Four at the coffee machine, a little reading while the baby is asleep, eating a meal or catching up on the news.

Then there are those activities, typically in the evening, which you consider to be your formal or dedicated rest activities—the bowling league, tying fishing flies, walking the dog, playing catch with Junior, watching the NCAA tournament.

So how long do you actually work? Considering all aspects of your work, I would generally say about twelve hours. Idlers work less, but diligent people put in roughly about twelve solid hours. So, giving you the benefit of the doubt, you are at best a half-time worker.

I'm not even going to respond to that.

And this only counts your "work" days. Usually you spend much more of the weekend on rest activities. My point is that you do not even come close to the six-to-one work-to-rest ratio. Nobody does.

But it's in the Bible!

Sabbath Re-examined

Look carefully at what actually is in the Bible.

> You shall keep the Sabbath, because it is holy for you. Everyone who profanes it shall be put to death. Whoever does any work on it, that soul shall be cut off from among his people. Six days shall work be done, but the seventh day is a Sabbath of solemn rest, holy to the LORD. Whoever does any work on the Sabbath day shall be put to death.
>
> Exodus 31:14-15

Two observations. First, remember that the Sabbath commandment was part of the Mosaic Law and was binding on the Jews under the Old Covenant. Considering the penalty, Christians

142

should be thankful to be under the New Covenant not the Old. You should be grateful that you are under grace not law, both as the basis of justification and as a rule of life. Second, Sabbath law prohibits work on the seventh day but does not prohibit rest on the first six days of the week. "Six days shall work be done" is a command to do work not a command that forbids rest. The Jews could rest every day and needed to just like the rest of us. The seventh day was "holy" because it was an *entire* day set apart from work days for a special observance of rest.

So the six-to-one ratio was a Covenantal requirement for Jews concerning the number of days in which work was to be done versus the day work was not to be done.

A Breakthrough in Rest Science!

Uh, excuse me! I thought that we were done with all the theology. And all you have managed to do so far is to not answer the question. What is the correct ratio of work to rest?

The answer is…it depends. There are many factors in play:

How intense is your work?

How refreshing is your rest?

How long has it been since your last deep, extended rest?

What is the burden of your accumulated stresses and burdens?

What are your current circumstances?

These questions reveal the fluidity of your rest requirement. It changes constantly.

Fortunately for you, I have invented a device to indicate when you are resting properly—the Rest-O-Meter! This is not an electrical or mechanical instrument but a conceptual one. If you have purchased this book, I grant you unlimited use of your own personal Rest-O-Meter. If you have borrowed or stolen this book, send me fifty bucks for usage rights.

Here it is:

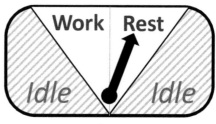

Rest-O-Meter

Your goal is to keep the needle of your Rest-O-Meter within the Work-Rest zone. If you do, you are living in balance. When you are in balance, the needle oscillates between your work and rest activities, like this:

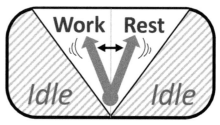

Rest-O-Meter

What are the benefits of being in work-rest balance? You will have good energy, a sense of humor, enthusiasm, fortitude, joy and a realistic perspective. You will be efficient and productive. You will work hard and obtain the corresponding rest that you need. You will have established good daily, weekly and yearly rest structures. During extraordinarily demanding or difficult times, you will have enough reserve to respond in a God-honoring way. As soon as circumstances allow, you will take expanded rest to regain the balance.

The Meter Defeaters

The Idle zones of your Rest-O-Meter indicate that your work-rest ratio is out of kilter. You can enter Idle from the right, by refusing to work, or from the left, by neglecting your rest. I'll describe how the meter operates in both circumstances.

When the needle moves right into Idle, here is the pattern of the classic sluggard. Even the sluggard does a minimal amount of work to earn his bread. When he stops working he requires a bit of rest. So far so good. But when it is time to return to work, the sluggard refuses to do so. In fact, he avoids work as long as possible. He is idling.

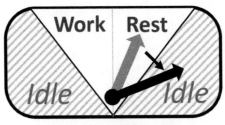

Rest-O-Meter

The simple cure for the sluggard is work. He needs more work to establish balance in his life.

But I suspect that this is not the pattern that you, friend, usually observe on your Rest-O-Meter. If you were a sluggard, I doubt you would be reading this book. I suspect that you are some variety of a workaholic. Your problem begins not with too little work but with too much. I will not review all of the theological, sociological and psychological reasons that you do this. The practical outcome is that you overwork and neglect rest until you achieve some level of exhaustion.

Think about your exhaustion. In this condition you have little energy and are usually short-tempered, obstinate and defensive. Despite your seemingly heroic labors, your work is not as productive as it should be because you are in an Exhaustion Spiral. Also, you are probably neglecting the family and church spheres of work. You are overwhelmed and your gas tank is nearly empty.

It is not as though you do not rest at all. Everyone must rest some. But just as the lazy sluggard works a little, the exhausted workaholic rests a little—the minimal sustainment level. Most workaholics rest enough to hold off insanity or death, but the more advanced the workaholism, the less the margin. In your case, you are probably only in the initial stages and are still functional.

I'm glad that you think so.

Well, I try to be fair. Here is what happens. You overwork and become exhausted. If you would engage in good rest activities at this point—ones that provide change and concentration—your Rest-O-Meter needle would be in the Rest area. But you don't engage in good rest activities. You tell yourself that you are too tired for such things and that you do not have time for them. Instead you do whatever takes the least amount of effort, such as playing games on your gizmo or watching television. The problem is that these types of activities provide meager refreshment value. You invest little and receive little in return.

Since you are still too tired to return to work and not willing to take the initiative for more productive rest, you continue with your paltry amusements. A little more time will do the trick, right? What you originally intended to be a quick break begins to stretch out. One hour turns into two…and then three…and then four. If you were not in such a fatigued condition, you would realize that you have spent as much—or more—time on the low-value activity as you could have on the high-value activity. The difference is, of course, that you have very little to show for your time investment. And since you are not refreshed *from* work, you are not ready to return *to* work. Ironically in your determination to keep your foot on the gas, you end up idling.

Here's a look at the meter:

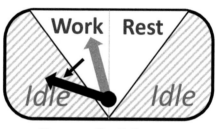

Rest-O-Meter

There is a parallel with eating. Say that you are hungry and have the choice of sitting down to a nice steak dinner or snacking on some chips. You say to yourself that you don't really need such an enjoyable and lengthy meal as a steak dinner. You can get by on less. After all, you are self-controlled, disciplined, focused. So you of grab a handful of chips. But that one handful does not satisfy your hunger, so you take another and another and another. You cannot seem to stop yourself until the whole big bag of chips is consumed. Now you are bloated but not really satisfied. You are also disgusted with yourself for your lack of self-control. Now what is your response? You vow to eat less to make up for your lapse. This results in more missed nutritious meals…followed by more junk food binges. Your good intentions have resulted in a very poor eating structure. The point? Eat well. And rest well.

Another point. Good resting is also the most efficient resting. There are no shortcuts to good resting. Your shortcuts will end up as longcuts. You will end up wasting your time by trying to reduce your rest below what you require. Be a good steward. Plan good rest activities. Check your Rest-O-Meter frequently and keep your needle oscillating between work and rest. The needle will constantly be moving as your circumstances change. You must make the corresponding adjustments to your activities.

Keep Your Eyes on Your Gauge

One last observation. Focus on *your* Rest-O-Meter. It is the only one uniquely calibrated to your condition. You will be tempted to try to swap yours for one that belongs to another person, someone you admire. Perhaps this is a prominent leader, a mentor, a friend, or a famous historical figure—someone that you imagine works harder and longer than you or can seemingly do it all, while needing little rest. You would rather have their Rest-O-Meter than your own. This is "meter envy" and it causes you to set an unachievable level of work for yourself.

Besides, these Rest-O-Meters are almost always illusory. Most people have about the same capacity for work and about the same need for an amount of rest. If someone is very productive in their work, it is usually because they have learned to become excellent resters. The thing is, you know about their work but not about their rest. Why? Because people usually talk about their work but seldom describe their rest. This is to be expected because their public work is the focus of attention, not their private rest.

If this is true for the living, it is worse for the dead. The dead are eulogized by admiring biographers who selectively focus on their most productive works. Any writer knows this is unavoidable. If a writer tells you everything about the person, it would just be a bunch of endless babbling without coming to some point. So with all the focus on impressive work, you assume that your heroes rested little.

Having said that, a few people are gifted with an extraordinary capacity for work. The Apostle Paul was one of them. He said so himself.

...I worked harder than any of them [the other apostles]....

I Corinthians 15:10

For you remember, brothers, our labor and toil: we worked night and day....

I Thessalonians 2:9

Three observations. First, Paul did not need to spend time providing for the needs of his family. Why? He was unmarried and this allowed him to focus most of his energy on ministry work. Second, when Paul said he "worked day and night" this is not to be taken literally, as if he never slept or rested in any way. He is making the point that he worked hard for the cause of Christ. You should work day and night too, just not *all* day and *all* night. Third, and most obviously, you are not Paul. You cannot trade your Rest-O-Meters for his, no matter how much you would like to. You are different people.

But I am to imitate Paul (Phillipians 3:17), aren't I?

Yes, certainly. But make a careful distinction here. You should follow Paul's example, but you should not try to mimic him (or anybody else). The difference is between attempting to replicate his virtues in your own life and attempting to *be* him. Like Paul, you should strive to work hard, have faith and persevere. But you cannot have his Rest-O-Meter. You are stuck with the one you have been given. Be faithful within your limits. This is what you are accountable for.

Your work-rest ratio is what it is. Learn to attune yourself to it.

CHAPTER TWENTY-ONE

Resting With God

I will now venture into the topic of devotions. This is your time for Bible reading and prayer. This activity is often referred to as "meeting with God." Generally it refers to a daily practice, but it may also include special activities, such as extended times in solitude. Devotional time is an intentional act on your part to focus on God. You are the one that requires the focusing. God is already quite good at it. He is ever present and all knowing. He is not distant or removed or disengaged and then suddenly comes near and becomes attentive when you beckon. No. You are concentrating on the One Who Is.

Devotional time consists both of listening to God speak, through his Word, and responding, through prayer. You know how essential this practice is to your Christian walk. The question is, what are you doing when you do it? Are you working or resting?

Where to begin? Since time with God is based upon relationship to God, I will start there.

In a Relationship

Before you repented of your sins and believed the Gospel you were an enemy of God, ungrateful and rebellious. But through faith in Jesus' life, death and resurrection, your relationship to God was completely changed. You went from the very worst position, which you deserved, to the very best, which you do not deserve. You did not earn this privilege by trying to be better but by receiving salvation as a gift, a most gracious and transforming gift. This truth is the core of

Christianity. I only mention it briefly here to remind you of your position in Christ.

> For if while we were enemies we were reconciled to God
> by the death of his Son, much more, now that we are
> reconciled, shall we be saved by his life.
>
> Romans 5:10

Consider some of the aspects of this new relationship.
I thought this was supposed to be about devotions?
Patience, friend.

King, Master and Lord

Every human being will eventually acknowledge that God is the rightful and only Ruler of the universe. It is not a question of *if* but of *when*. A Christian enjoys the blessing of submitting to his Kingship now, prior to the final judgment. He is your Master and Lord. You are willingly his servant and steward.

The New Testament describes the various roles you are to fulfill in this relationship. One is soldier. You are fighting a great spiritual battle. A second role is builder. You are constructing the Church brick upon brick. A third is farmer. You sow and harvest the fields of the Kingdom of God. In each of these roles—the soldier, the builder, the farmer—the Bible and prayer are indispensable. They are the weapons of war, the tools of construction, seed for the sower and water for the grower. In short, they are the means of accomplishing ministry.

And what is ministry? It is work. When you fight, build and farm you are serving your King, Master and Lord, just as you are serving him in all spheres of your work. But what about a change from work? How do you interact with God in rest?

Father, Brother, Friend

In addition to the blessing of working for the Best Boss, you have an even greater privilege. Your relationship to God is described in the more intimate terms of family and friendship. You have the indescribable honor of addressing the Creator God as Father. Think of that! Jesus taught you to pray, "Our Father in heaven...." He prayed "Abba, Father" at Gethsemane and you are to pray the same way.

> For you did not receive the spirit of slavery to fall back
> into fear, but you have received the Spirit of adoption as
> sons, by whom we cry, "Abba! Father!"
>
> Romans 8:15

If the fatherhood of God is not astounding enough, you also know God the Son in a very personal way. Jesus is your brother and friend.

> For those whom he foreknew he also predestined to be
> conformed to the image of his Son, in order that he might
> be the firstborn among many brothers.
>
> Romans 8:29

> You are my friends if you do what I command you. No
> longer do I call you servants, for the servant does not
> know what his master is doing; but I have called you
> friends, for all that I have heard from my Father I have
> made known to you.
>
> John 15:14-15

While the king/master/lord relationship brings to mind honor, respect and service, the father/brother/friend relationship evokes privilege, affection and closeness. You petition the King, but you bare your heart to your Father. You obey your Master, but you enjoy your Brother. You follow your Lord, but you confide in your Friend.

I see where you are going with this. I am supposed to constantly evaluate how I am relating to God—at this instance as King and in the next as Father, or now to Jesus as Brother but then as Lord? Really, what difference does it make? Aren't I supposed to relate to God in all of these ways?

Yes, of course. These relationships are inseparable. God is not your King *or* your Father. He is always your Father-King. Jesus is your Lord-Brother and Friend-Master. My point is simply that you relate to God in a number of ways, not just as his workers.

And what does this have to do with my devotional time?

Just this—you need to spend time with God in rest. Relationship involves sharing together in both work and rest. If you will remember, I touched on this point earlier in the context of the child-parent relationship. Parenting is not an endless exercise of work—at least it had better not be! Children are not merely a "job." No. A parent should relate to a child through both work and rest activities, just as Jesus interacted with his disciples through work and rest activities.

151

Relationship spans across all that you do.

Now let me ask you a question. Do you rest with God?

Well, as you said, I read the Bible and pray during my devotions.

How do you read the Bible? What is the purpose of your reading?

I am studying the book of James now.

You are "studying." Like studying for a test?

Do you think I'm in seminary? Not! I am leading a Bible study in James.

I see. You use your devotion time to prepare for the Bible study.

Correct.

Okay. Leading a Bible study is ministry. Ministry is work. Preparing for ministry is part of the work of ministry. You are working during your devotional time.

I never really thought of it that way before.

I know. Now let's move on to prayer.

Do we have to?

Please. Everyone needs to hear this. How do you pray? What is your purpose for praying?

I pray through my prayer list. Do you have a problem with that?

Certainly not. You are to be commended. So then, you are praying for the needs of others?

Yes, for my family, my church, missionaries, persecuted believers, unbelievers, our leaders—not "name it and claim it" type of prayers, but for God's will to be done.

Would you say that you are "ministering" to others through your prayers?

I guess so. Does this mean that I am working again?

Of course.

But what is wrong with it?

Nothing. All Christians should pray for God's people and for his will to be done. But realize that you are meeting with God to work. You are approaching him as King/Lord/Master. But do you regularly approach him as Father/Brother/Friend? You work for God, but do you rest with him? Do you ever spend time with him simply for the joy of it, for fellowship and companionship? Or is your focus only to get some work done and then move on to your next task?

Ironically, many sincere Christians consider Bible reading and prayer to be their only time of "true rest" when actually they are not resting at all. They are fully absorbed in ministry work. You fit into this category, don't you? You draw near to the King in order to take care of business. You never set aside your armor, your hammer and your hoe. No. You labor on and on and on. Compulsively. You are always a Martha. Never a Mary. It is no wonder you are exhausted.

Now you are piling on.

Uncommon Grace

Every human being may partake of all the other rest activities I am describing in this book. They are yours—and everybody else's—by right of descent from Adam. They are common blessings to the human race. I have been making the case that these expressions of rest are just as important for the well-being of the Christian as for the unbeliever. I am simply reminding you of the obvious fact that you are still human. You did not shed your humanity upon being born again.

But resting with God is the unique privilege of the Christian. Adam's race lost this privilege upon Adam's fall. Those born of Adam are separated from God. All were kicked out of the Garden with Adam and away from a closeness to God. But what was lost in Adam is restored in Christ.

To think about how important this aspect of rest is, consider how the unbeliever attempts to fill this hole in his experience. He refuses to draw near to his Creator in repentance. Instead, he may fashion a god more to his liking. This project may involve joining with others in a religious commitment or may take some form of a personal spiritual quest. The problem is, in either case, that there can be no relationship with a god who does not exist. Or the unbeliever may seek to fulfill his longing through communion with nature. "Nature" is code for creation without acknowledging the Creator. But there can be no personal relationship with that which is impersonal, no matter how magnificent it is. Creation points to the Creator. It does not replace him. Or the unbeliever may attempt to cover his longing for God by seeking fulfillment in experience. The folly here is obvious too. All of these fall short. They can never provide the full God-centered rest that all people need.

But you—Christian—have both the privilege and opportunity to partake of this rest. Do you?

The End of the Matter

I understand what you are saying, but I'm having a difficult time with your distinction between "working for God" and "resting with God." This seems legalistic to me. In my best and most intimate fellowship with God, I naturally pray for myself and others. But, according to you, this is work and should not be mixed with rest. Are you saying that I need to have a devotional time of rest and have separate times for prayer and Bible study?

I am not advocating a work/rest legalism. Strict separation is impossible. But I recommend that you evaluate whether you are primarily working or resting during your devotional time. How do you tell the difference? That is simple. Are you refreshed because you have rested or are you in need of refreshment because you have labored? If that question does not ring the bell for you, here is another: When you have finished devotions are you ready to begin work or do you need a little time (i.e. rest) before exerting yourself in your next work task?

Serve God in all things, of course, but also rest with him. Engage him in all aspects of your relationship with him. Read his word for pleasure, for the joy of it. Respond intimately in praise and worship and obedience. Pour out your heart before him. Lay your burdens at his feet. Take shelter under his wings. Find your strength and comfort and restitution in him. Enjoy him. Drink deeply of him and be refreshed.

CHAPTER TWENTY-TWO

Lower Your Expectations

The quickest way to ruin something pretty good is to expect it to be perfect. This is as true for rest as it is for work. But since there is more biblical light about work, I will examine it first. Then I will draw a parallel with rest.

I weary of all of your drawing of parallels and metaphors and endless examples! Give me a break! Why can't you just say something straight out? Why do you have to explain something by referring to something else? I'm going to snap!

Calm yourself, friend. You learn best by relating the obscure to the clear, by linking what you do not know to what you know. Also, this book will only be useful if you actually *become* a better rester. To become one, you need to wrestle with these ideas, to fully digest them…oops, more metaphors. Anyway if you have read this far, you might as well finish. Take a deep breath. Think about a cabin for a moment.

Ready to proceed? Good. The crisis passes.

Back to Work

Work is part of the created order. God works. His work reflects his being, his character, his purpose and his plan. God's work is completely good. But that is no longer true for us. The Bible tells us that something has tainted our work. Sin.

> And to Adam he said, "Because you have listened to the voice of your wife and have eaten of the tree of which I commanded you, 'You shall not eat of it,' cursed is the ground because of you; in pain you shall eat of it all the

days of your life; thorns and thistles it shall bring forth for
you; and you shall eat the plants of the field. By the sweat
of your face you shall eat bread, till you return to the
ground, for out of it you were taken; for you are dust, and
to dust you shall return."

Genesis 3:17-19

Because of the fall, man's work is now corrupted. It is toilsome.
You must sweat in order to earn your bread. Work is painful. You get
pricked by thorns and thistles in your labors. *This shouldn't be so hard! I
enjoy the work, it's the people I can't stand! We need better customers! My boss
doesn't have a clue! I am being taken advantage of! Everything is against me!* This
is unpleasant, but it does not mean that you cease work. The created
work-rest order is still intact. Someone still needs to pick the
apples...even though the apples are imperfect and some of them are
rotten. Furthermore, you are commanded to glorify God through your
apple picking. To put it simply, you should do the best you can given
the situation.

Live To Work or Work to Live?

You should not be surprised that those who reject God's explanation
for what's wrong in the world will attempt to deny it at every turn. This
is certainly true for work. One of the follies of denying the reality of
sin is to expect too much from work, that is, to find "fulfillment" in
work. This goes beyond gratification for a job well done. I am using
"fulfillment" in the sense of work being the purpose of life. That is,
work becomes an end in itself not merely the means to an end.

Not all unbelievers are trying to find meaning in their work. Because
of the toilsomeness of work some have given up on it and look
elsewhere. Where do they look? To rest, of course. The work idol is
unsatisfying, so they fashion another out of rest. This may take the
form of dedication to a sport, a hobby or a club. It may find expression
in interests such as travel or reading or being a fan of a team. While
these things may be useful rest activities, like work they fall far short
of being the reason for existence.

For those who live solely for themselves, work or rest may become
a form of self-actualization, that is, an attempt fulfill their potential.
Potential for what? Who knows? In any case, this is choosing the
molehill over the mountain.

Work and rest are simply too small to provide meaning. Fulfillment can only be found in something—or rather some*one*—much bigger. That would be Jesus.

> For by him all things were created, in heaven and on earth, visible and invisible, whether thrones or dominions or rulers or authorities—all things were created through him and for him. And he is before all things, and in him all things hold together. And he is the head of the body, the church. He is the beginning, the firstborn from the dead, that in everything he might be preeminent.
>
> Colossians 1:16-18

When you willingly honor the Lord Christ through your work and rest, you are acknowledging his supremacy. You are cooperating with reality instead of resisting it. When your aim is to glorify Jesus, you are properly aligned with your purpose for existing. Or as Jesus said in his paradoxical way: "For whoever would save his life will lose it, but whoever loses his life for my sake will find it" (Matthew 16:25).

Frustration Continuation

Christians should know these things. And you should not be surprised when work is toilsome, but sometimes you are. This may be because you really think God exists to serve you instead of the other way around. *Why isn't God making everything happy for me?* Or it may be because your theology gets plugged up in your head and never drains down to your hands and feet. You do not connect the dots between theory and application. *Oh, I have to experience the curse too?* Or you may imagine a fantasy "dream job" and chase it, like a mirage, from one occupation to another.

You are never content, so you wallow in a bog of bitterness and complaining. You should, of course, improve your work situation when possible. It is a matter of stewardship to use your gifts and abilities fully and to earn more in order to meet more needs. But you need to remember that you are to glorify God right now through whatever work you have.

You will be more willing to do this when you expect to experience a level of frustration in your work.

Just as work is disappointing, so is rest. You often expect too much from your rest. You swallow the advertising hype, the overly enthusiastic recommendations, or the unrealistic expectations of your own imaginations. But actual rest falls short, such as in these testimonials:

> *So much for our trip to "paradise." Fred was crabby after the flight and he never got used to the time change. I ate a bad mango and it spoiled my regularity for the rest of the week.*
>
> Ethel

> *I dunno. That was supposed to be a really good novel, but I said to myself, "Not so much." The plot seemed pretty stupid and I thought that the main guy was a jerk.*
>
> Ollie

> *Going to a nice restaurant was supposed to be a special treat for the family. But I could tell that Jim's thoughts were still at work. Then Little Missy spilled her drink and Junior thought it was funny. He got into one of his laughing fits until the tears flowed from his eyes and he snorted some mashed potatoes out of his nose. I was so embarrassed!*
>
> Julia

> *I was enjoying the solitude while re-plumbing the cabin, but the crawl space was mighty narrow and I gave my noggin three or four pretty good thumps on the floor joists. I think that I knocked myself out one of those times.*
>
> Bob

> *Everyone was looking forward to the camping trip. As usual, the weather man was wrong. It started raining when we got there and kept on – a hard, steady rain. At 1 a.m. we realized that the tent was leaking and our sleeping bags were soaked. We decided to play cards. It was a long night.*
>
> Marigold

Surprised By Joy

These type of things happen. You should expect them. Rest is as tarnished as work in this fallen world. And yet Christians are to be characterized by joy (Galatians 5:22). How do you reconcile this seeming contradiction—the effects of sin and an attitude of joy?

You cannot always reconcile these, but you can hold on to both truths. You have two hands. Do not drop what is in the right when you grasp something else with the left. If you are a whiner, always focused on and complaining about the frustrations in life, you are not holding on to joy in the Lord. You are forgetting that God is working all things for good, even things that are not good in themselves. On the other hand, if you refuse to acknowledge the disappointments that you experience, you are minimizing the realities of life in a fallen world. You are kidding yourself. Keep a firm grip with both hands.

When you do, you will be able to enjoy your rest (as well as your work) to the fullest extent possible. And there is a bonus to the difficulties you encounter in rest activities. They make things interesting. As a result, you will remember them. And, in time, you may even come to enjoy them.

Picture a family reunion or guys sitting around swapping stories or a young man revealing something about himself to an interested young lady. Not one of them is going to be talking about good weather, the easy hike, or their well-behaved siblings. No. They will be telling stories about playing cards all night in the tent, getting lost on that hike, and snorting those mashed potatoes. This is rest seasoned with adversity. It's really not so bad, and it gets better with age. So learn to take things in stride.

Regarding the lousy novel, we will discuss that in the next chapter.

Ending on a High Note

Originally this was going to be the last chapter of this book. A final caution, so to speak. But then I thought: *How stupid to end with the shortcomings of rest! After all, I am trying to encourage people to rest not discourage them. Instead I will conclude the practical theory section with it.* And so I have.

There is one more reason to put this chapter here. The next and final section is about the application of rest. It is my recommendation of specific rest activities. Naturally these are my favorites and I am enthused about them. So now I can cut loose and pitch my recommendations to you without restraint. You will see no tiresome qualifiers. *You are bound to be disappointed at some point. Don't anticipate too much. You will never experience that level of thrill and excitement again.* No, I will write none of this. You will need to remind yourself that rest will never be perfect and you should not expect it to be.

PART III

The Experience of Rest

For the practice of rest, I've only shown theory.
So your mind is befuddled, your eyesight is bleary.

Enough of this labor—it is time for some fun!
The last of this book is what I have done.

Now I beg you, dear reader, to press to the end.
My reason has ended, my stories I lend.

I'll start with reading, this is a fine rest.
Nurture this pleasure and you will be blest.

Sporting activities should not be despised.
The elements of rest are well exercised.

Travel and find new worlds for exploring.
Strap on a backpack and go out-of-dooring.

So many good gifts, which one is the best?
Ah…all come together in the cabin of rest.

Reading for Pleasure

I never read a book for rest until I was thirty-one years old. My wife Lori and I had just bought our first little house. There was a pile of stuff on the porch left over from the seller's garage sale. I was not interested in much of it, but one of the paperbacks caught my attention—*The Hunt for Red October* by Tom Clancy.

But I did not read for rest. I would not have described it that way— read for rest—back then. I would have used the more common terminology. I did not "read for pleasure," which is a very apt phrase. This means reading simply for the joy and delight of it. No, not me. I read only for work. Reading anything else, I reasoned, was a waste of precious time. So were any other frivolous doings (a.k.a. rest activities). This sounds like I was very disciplined and serious. I'm sure most people thought so and were impressed with me. I certainly was.

But for some reason—weakness or a character flaw, no doubt—I started to read *The Hunt for Red October*. My misinformed conscience generated nagging and unnecessary guilt, but the story captivated me and I had to keep reading. Here was excitement and intrigue. In addition, I was learning about submarine warfare and the CIA. *Isn't it important for Christians to understand what is happening in the world? Sure it is. This knowledge may open a door for evangelism. Hmmm. That's a bit of a stretch.* Despite my internal struggles, I really enjoyed reading that book. I had to find out if Jack Ryan could pull it off?

Jack pulled it off, of course, but I discovered something more important. Reading can be a source of satisfying and enriching rest. Reading can refresh.

Of course, it can also exhaust.

Reading for Work

The purpose of all reading is to learn something you do not know. If you already knew what you were going to read, there would be no point in reading about it. This is true for both work and rest reading. You always read to learn.

The distinction between work reading and rest reading lies in the content of what you read and the style of how you read. I will consider these characteristics for both work and rest. I begin with work because work always precedes rest and establishes what rest is not. And there is one more reason to consider work reading first. Most people are very familiar with this type of reading, while fewer and fewer know how to read for pleasure.

So off to work. You need information to accomplish work because work always involves knowledge. You must know what you are doing in order to produce something. That something may be a marketing strategy, a sermon illustration, remodeling a house, internet security, better gas mileage, or a new meal for dinner. The information you need is buried in messages, reports, instructions, studies, articles, briefings, regulations, etc. This type of information is the *content* of work reading.

Now for the style of work reading. This can best be described as "data mining." You search for particular information, and when you locate it you dig it out and use it. Since you strive for efficiency at work, the sooner you retrieve and utilize the information the better. Our goal is to spend as little time reading as possible so that you may move to the next phase of the task.

So then in both content and style, work reading is strictly utilitarian. Its purpose is to obtain the information required to accomplish work. My point is not to denigrate work reading, only to characterize it properly. Work reading is valuable and necessary…for work. Also, I am not implying that work reading is always dull and onerous. If you are interested in your work, which I hope you are, you will find the reading related to it interesting also.

Traumatized at School

However, there is one subset of work reading that most people find dull and onerous. School reading. School reading is work because schooling is the work of preparing for work. There are two reasons most people do not enjoy school reading. The first is that it involves the reading of textbooks. Textbooks consolidate information on a subject efficiently, but they do so in an extremely unimaginative and tedious way. Take history textbooks, for example. These strip the *story* out of history and reduce the narrative to facts. Boring!

Do you think that I am being too harsh? Well, when was the last time you read through your old college textbooks? Uh-huh. Never. You probably held on to them for a few years and then donated them to a charity, which would be stuck with disposing of them after not being able to sell them. Fewer and fewer students are even reading their textbooks when they are forced to, that is for class, so I doubt they will be reading them for pleasure.

This brings me to the second reason school reading is dull and onerous. Although students avoid reading their textbooks if at all possible, at times they may be forced into it in order to pass a test. This is actually good training for work reading because they learn to extract the necessary information with the least amount of effort. A student develops the art of rapid scanning. But unlike other work reading where the reader knows there is a useful purpose for the information, the student's objective is only to cram down the data and regurgitate it on the test. He develops a habit of textbook bulimia—binging on the data just prior to the test and then purging during the test. This is an unpleasant experience.

I don't know how you wandered into this rant, but you have gone too far! You are criticizing education!

No, I am very fond of education. I am criticizing schooling.

I see. You were a poor student and couldn't keep up. You were traumatized in the academic milieu, and now you are striking back.

Actually, I was an excellent student. I just didn't learn anything.

I can understand why that happened.

Let's stop this snipping. My point is that the reading experience is shaped by school reading, in particular, and work reading, in general. This is a utilitarian, data mining, scanning type of reading. It is reading mandated by necessity. Because of these associations, many people refuse to read for pleasure or have never seriously considered the possibility. Perhaps you are one of them. If so, you are missing out on a completely different reading experience.

How is reading for rest different? I will answer this question using Mr. Churchill's change and concentration criteria.

Change

Reading for rest must provide change from work. An immediate objection arises, which I have heard many times. Go ahead and say it.

Since I read for work, I do not want to read for rest.

At first blush this appears to be an appropriate application of the change principle. But there is a flaw in this reasoning. You assumes that all reading is reading, without distinction. But there are important distinctions. To see them, substitute "walking" for resting. Would you insist that you could not walk for rest if you walk for work? *I walk throughout the day at the office, doing this and that, so I could not possibly find rest by walking in the park in the evening, watching the children play, listening to the birds, enjoying the feel of the weather....* When I put it like that, walking is obviously a means of either work or rest. So is reading. Satire helps make this clear. I hope you enjoyed it because I've got some more.

There is another error when it comes to rest and reading. Instead of assuming that rest reading will be work, this fallacy assumes that work reading will be rest. More specifically, it assumes that work reading not done *at* work will provide rest. This seems to be largely a failing among men. Women generally have a knack for recognizing this numbskullery. But not some men. Engineers read studies. Managers read business books. Marketeers read about advertising. When I encounter this, I make a mental note. *This guy does not read for rest, is most likely a workaholic, and is probably as interesting as a brick.* Speaking of bricks, if he were a mason he would be laying bricks in the evening after laying bricks all day on the job. Is this change? No. Refreshment? No. More work does not provide rejuvenation from work.

So the key to reading for rest is reading something different than work reading. What is that? Anything else. The alternatives are nearly endless. Here are a few ideas:

Napoleonic era sea fiction

The horrors of the Soviet prison system

Stories of clueless rich young Englishmen and their brilliant manservants

Scouting eastern Siberia in the 1860s for a transcontinental telegraph route

The place of hobbits, quests, friendship and sacrifice

These describe a few of my favorites. Whenever I enter into one of these worlds through a book, I leave my work far behind. That is the point.

Enriching Refreshment

What kind of reading provides the best rest? That is a question I can answer for me but not for you. Your work is different than mine, so your not-work will be different than mine. Also, your interests are different than mine. These differences will lead to unique reading lists. However, I have one recommendation. Read widely. Broaden your horizons. Cast a large net. Do not settle into one genre or historical period or topic. Cultivate new interests. Like all of the best rest activities, good reading will deeply enrich and broaden you. You will become more knowledgeable and more reflective. As your discernment matures, read an author that you disagree with. Take his best shot and refute him…or perhaps adjust your own position.

Good reading is not amusement, that is, a mindless and trivial distraction. Good reading is musement, a careful and thoughtful consideration of something. I am not suggesting that you should trudge through the "classics" or academic tomes. This may impress others, but it is often the worst approach for nurturing a love for rest reading. Find what *you* enjoy. This may be history, biography, story or reading related to your other rest interests.

True Fiction and Good Sex

While all reading increases your knowledge, one category of reading especially increases your knowledge of yourself and others. Fiction. At this point I have a disclaimer. I take fiction so seriously and believe that it can be so beneficial that I have taken the pains to write some myself.

I suspected that! You must be referring to writings in addition to this book, which seems to be mostly fiction to me. So answer this, Cabin Man. Why should I waste my time reading something that is not real? Shouldn't I be spending my rest time on something more profitable?

Let me ask you something in return. Are Jesus' parables real? They are not if "real" means the stories occurred in the physical realm by living human beings just as narrated. Do you dismiss them because they are not "real?" Of course not. A better question is this, "Is the story true?" All of Jesus' parables are profoundly true. That is, they reflect and illustrate the realities of God's moral universe. Of course, not all fiction—or all non-fiction, for that matter—is true. Some is false, a lie. It is your responsibility as the reader to discern which is which.

For example, consider sex. There is a great popular lie that sex is always good...if consensual and compelled by romantic feelings. The Bible teaches us not to be so dimwitted. Sex between a man and woman in marriage is good and is a great blessing. All other sex is sinful. Now if a male character is fornicating with every attractive female—or vice versa—that comes across his or her path and this is presented as desirable and fulfilling and without negative consequences, then here is a lie. Sin always brings misery and all of the lying stories in the world will not change this. This is immoral fiction. On the other hand, if fornication is portrayed as foolishness and natural painful consequences follow, then the story is moral.

If you have not noticed, the Bible is full of sex. There is good sex, such in the marriage of Isaac and Rebecca or Boaz and Ruth. And then there is the other kind. Remember the sordid tales of Judah and Tamar, Sampson and Delilah, and David and Bathsheba? All of these portrayals are moral. They teach us to love what is good and despise what is evil. Also, the narratives are not explicit. They do not describe sexual acts in a way that tempts us to lust. Of course, the Song of Solomon gets a little juicy. I do not recommend that single people linger over some of these passages and, if you are married, only do so with your spouse in mind.

The most subtle aspects of fiction are its underlying messages and assumptions. Do not focus only on the brazen—sex, violence and language—and miss the message. This is especially important with children's or G-rated literature. You drop your discernment because you assume that it must be "wholesome." Instead, immorality is often hidden within like weevils in the biscuits.

Follow your heart
Be true to yourself
You can be anything you want to be
The ends justifies the means

At this point you may be thinking about movies. While few read books consistently, almost everyone watches movies or other electronic entertainment. In addition to sports, it is one of the last vestiges of common culture. Whether for books or movies, you should become more and more discerning of the content you consume.

And you should avoid content that leads you into temptation. Godliness demands this, but so does restfulness. Sin corrupts everything it touches. Sin ruins rest. Why? Because sin brings guilt. And guilt drains the joy out of rest. And joyless rest provides little refreshment. Even if you confess, which I trust that you will, your sin will have spoiled your rest.

All of this to say that dangers lurk in works of fiction because they engage the imagination through entering the thoughts and actions of the characters. But just as imagination has the power to corrupt our thoughts, so too can it cleanse them by depicting what is true, noble, right, pure, lovely and admirable.

Concentration

Now for Mr. Churchill's second characteristic of good rest—concentration. By concentration he meant deep immersion into an activity. Full absorption. Prolonged focus. These phrases describe perfectly the style of reading appropriate for rest reading. Hopefully you can remember an experience when a book completely captivated you. You could not stop reading because you had to find out what would happen and how it would happen. It was not just the facts of the story but the telling of the story that delighted you. You fell into the pages and work was out of mind. That's the idea.

There is another thing about this kind of reading that is very important—a fringe benefit, so to speak. Deep reading instills the mental habit of concentration. Every time you dive between the covers of a book, you strengthen this habit. Reading for rest is a natural antidote to…

Oh, please! Not the soapbox again!

…to the scatterbrain habit of mind that you reinforce through the constant use of your gizmos. Focused reading is the cure for your short, jumpy attention span.

But there is an even more important reason to develop the skill of deep reading. What is it? The Bible. Since I already have addressed reading the Bible for rest, I will only mention it briefly here. You should regularly and thoughtfully read God's Word. The better rest reader you are in general will help you become a better reader of the Bible in particular because you become practiced in reading carefully. All of the best rest activities train us in the art of concentration, but reading should be especially important to Christians who are "People of The Book."

Speaking of books, are books the only medium for rest reading? No, of course not. Newspapers, magazines and many other formats may be sources of rest reading. But I propose that books are the best format. Why? Because they provide a sustained treatment of a subject or they tell long, involved, complex stories. Reading shorter blurbs, rapidly jumping from one to the next, is more the style of work reading. You have to concentrate more to read a book, which makes it better rest.

Structural Impediments

If I have convinced you to become a better rest reader, the next question is how do you do that? How do you build rest reading into your structure?

Out of all the rest activities that I am recommending, rest reading is both the easiest and the hardest to establish as a habit. Why? Because it is so accessible. You can always open a book. Or you can always do something else instead. Other rest activities, such as traveling or sports, require planning, coordination and the involvement of others. Once you have committed to them, they are self-reinforcing structures. This is not so with reading. You are in it alone. In fact, you must be alone. Personal reading requires a measure of solitude. Solitude is something that is disturbed by…well…everything. Here is the cry of the distracted reader. *Everything is against me! Give me a moment's peace with my book!*

These things do not make reading for rest impossible. They just mean that you must exercise a little determination. This begins with developing an appetite.

An Acquired Taste

Reading, like all finer pleasures in life, is an acquired taste. No one pops out of the womb screaming, "Give me Tolstoy or I shall die!" No. A love for reading begins with a desire to know and enjoy something. That something may be a witty and humorous story, the history of the Reformation, or how to actually catch fish when you go fishing. If you are not curious, you will not read for long. You probably will not even begin.

But I will assume that you are curious. You are obviously curious about rest because you are reading this book. That is a start. Now how can you expand your reading interests and find other books that will be restful and refreshing for you? Here is my advice. Begin by seeking out the recommendations of others. These may be reviews or reading lists. Just as for movie reviewers, find book reviewers that you trust. If a movie reviewer keeps giving thumbs up to stinkers, you should dismiss their recommendations. The same holds for book reviewers. If one gives you a good lead, their next recommendation will probably be good too.

Better yet, become a "book talker." That is, talk with your friends and acquaintances about books. It is not hard. Try this. *Have you read any good books lately?* It is a simple question and you will learn much about a person by asking it. And you may get a good book tip.

Book Time

After you have a collection of books you want to read, the next step is to find time to read them. You must establish habits of reading. This means that at certain times of the day, week and year you will regularly take up and read.

For many, including myself, the best daily time for rest reading is at night just before bed. Not only is it the best way to put aside my work and troubles, it is also a reward that I look forward to. No matter what has happened, the day ends well for me and I sleep soundly.

As for the time structures of weeks and years, certain days of the week may provide opportunities for extended reading, as do holidays and vacations. For me, cabin visits offer the rugged Rocky Mountains to explore outside the doors and every other possible time and place inside…between the covers of a good book. Fire crackling, cup of coffee, soft recliner, book in hand. Rest.

I have been rhapsodizing about personal reading, but now let me say a word about reading out loud with others. This makes reading a shared experience. When my children were young we read as a family nearly every night. This was our structure. It was what we did as a matter of course. Over the years we read lots of books—*The Little House on the Prairie*, *Little Britches*, *Narnia*, and *The Lord of the Rings*, to name a few of our favorite series. Family reading was a two-fold blessing. Not only did we enjoy the great stories, but they also bound us together in common imagination and memories.

Our children are now grown and have moved out of the house. But we have re-established the tradition of family reading at the cabin. When we gather at the cabin, we read together after dinner. If you are our guest at the cabin, you will join us. It is an important part of the rest experience.

Read, friend, for pleasure.

CHAPTER TWENTY-FOUR

Get in the Game

Not everyone enjoys sports. Are you one of them? Perhaps you were always the last one to be chosen for a team or a softball hit you in the nose during gym class. Or your distain may not be rooted in humiliation but reason. Sports too easily becomes an obsession or leads into a slough of idleness, you say. These are real dangers and many have fallen into them. But just because something is sometimes misused does not mean it should never be used. If you dislike sports, fine. Stop reading here and move on to the next chapter. Sports will not provide profitable rest for you unless you change your attitude.

But most people enjoy sports. I am one. If you are another, then consider how to most benefit from these activities. All rest activities must be cultivated to provide a good crop of refreshment.

There are two ways to engage in sports—playing and watching. I'll start with playing.

Play Ball!

Playing—that is the terminology usually used to describe participation in sports. *Do you play football? Do you play hockey?* "Play" is a good and appropriate word when sports provides recreation. And recreation is just another word for rest.

But not everyone engaged in sports is playing. As I have mentioned before, the professionals—those who earn their bread through sports—are working. This is obvious for multi-million-dollar celebrity athletes, but not so obvious for those lower on the food chain. College athletes on a scholarship are also working. So are the multitudes that aspire to earn scholarships or are striving to break into the professional ranks one way or the other. They are all working not resting.

But you are not interested in sports work. You are interested in refreshment from your work. Playing sports provides excellent refreshment because it involves the attributes of change and concentration.

Change is self-evident. You are doing something very different from your work if you are playing basketball or tennis or volleyball or bowling. This is certainly true for those whose jobs involve little physical activity, such as technical writers or air traffic controllers. But it may also be true for those whose jobs are more strenuous, such as mechanics or those who labor in retail or food service. The motions and exertions required in a game of racquetball are entirely different from any of the jobs listed above and may be just what is needed to blow off a little steam.

If change is good in sports, concentration is even better. Playing sports focuses you on the score, your opponents, your teammates, the conditions, your emotions and the time, to name a few of the elements. Sports competition is thoroughly absorbing. It fully occupies the mind just as it does the body. If your thoughts happen to drift back to work—*I wonder if Alice filed that subpoena?*—your teammates or your coach will soon have a word of encouragement for you. *Get your head in the game!* And they are right. Your head needs to be in the game if the rest of you is there. Otherwise, don't bother.

Couch Potato Athlete

Playing sports can provide quality rest, but what about watching sports? Is being a spectator as good as being a participant? Hmmm. Perhaps this is not a useful comparison. It is like asking, "Is a screwdriver or a hammer the better tool?" They are different things with different qualities. But both are useful.

Watching sports lacks physical exertion, but may still provide change by taking your mind off of work and focusing it on something interesting. That is the key—interest. Do you want to find out what will happen?

Years ago I visited a family in Germany. My friend invited me to a professional soccer game. When we arrived at the stadium I immediately noticed something unusual. "Where are the seats?" I asked. "There are none. You stand," he replied. At the time I knew nothing about soccer. I had only accepted the invitation out of politeness. I thought I was in for several long, uncomfortable, boring hours. Then my friend began to explain the rules of the game to me. He told me about the team, the players, the rivalry, the coach, and on and on. Before long I was yelling like all of those Germans. I got into the game because I knew something about it. Because I knew about it, I found it interesting. Because it was interesting, I fully concentrated on the game.

The Great Drama

Since the sports poo-pooers have stopped reading this chapter, let's talk about them. Between us, they just do not appreciate all the aspects of a sporting event. *That's just a bunch of overgrown men running back and forth. Big deal—they're trying to knock that little ball into a cup! How many times do the cars go around the same track?* To them it is all a bunch of nonsense that we simple yokels enjoy.

But there is drama in all of it. The goal is simple. Win. But winning is hard. It requires brains and sweat and strategy and adjustments and cooperation and failure. And the greater the obstacles and opposition, the sweeter the victory in the end.

Hmmm. The last paragraph would be a pretty good description of the Christian life, wouldn't it? That is because sports illustrates the great unseen eternal drama. This is not my observation. The Apostle Paul used several sports metaphors for this purpose. I'm with Paul on this one. You should be too.

Anger Management

If you want to enjoy sports, you have to pick sides. You must commit. You need to have an emotional investment in your team. You need skin in the game so that you care about who wins and who loses.

There is risk here, of course. You risk disappointment. Your team may not win. In fact, your team may be the biggest perennial loser in the league. They may be loaded with talent and show great promise at the beginning of the season...and then collapse at the critical moment...again. How many times can your heart be broken? Well, lots. Seventy times seven would be a good estimate. That is okay. Learn to be faithful to your team. Persevere.

But there are many who do not have this attitude. Some get mad. Are you one of them? If you complain about the officials, yell at the players and coaches, boo, hiss, pray imprecatory prayers, grind your teeth, throw things onto the floor, or basically behave like a two-year old, then I have a word of advice. Sports is not a good rest activity for you, whether you are playing or watching. Give it up. You lack self-control in this area. Your anger and frustration is sin. And sin always taints rest and makes it less refreshing.

I am not saying that you should be happy about losing. Only an insane person or an athlete blackmailed by the mob finds satisfaction in a loss. Instead I am suggesting that you become somewhat philosophical about the situation. *After all, it is just a game. We are rebuilding. There is always next year.* That's the spirit! Win or lose, you should learn to be content with the outcome and be thankful for the rest you have received.

Water Cooler Talk

One more thing. There is another benefit to sports. It is truly one of the last vestiges of common culture. That is, sports gives you something to talk to others about. Is it the most important thing to talk about? No, of course not. But sports provides a point of shared experience. It is a place to start. It is, let me say, a "gateway drug" to conversation that may open the door to more serious topics with your fellow citizens.

And even if it does not, a little sports chatter provides a bit of refreshment, like a breeze on a hot day.

CHAPTER TWENTY-FIVE

Going Somewhere Else

Rest comes in different doses. You get a small dose when you take a moment to do something like step away from the computer and stretch our legs or have a chat with a friend about the weekend. You get a medium dose when you have a good long read or spend a holiday at the cabin. At times, especially when your work has been intense, you need a large dose. You need deep restorative prolonged rest.

Traveling is one of the best ways to obtain this level of rest. The two essential elements of rest—change and concentration—are inherent in traveling. Travel, by definition, means going to some place different and doing different things. It entails both a change of location and agenda. There is different scenery, different people and different history to explore. A good traveler becomes immersed in all these elements in order to fully experience the journey. That is, a good traveler concentrates on his travels. He leaves his work far behind in a distant land.

But just because travel is inherently restful does not mean that you cannot spoil the opportunity. Becoming a good traveler is a learned art, as are all rest practices. Going on a trip no more guarantees rest than buying a fishing pole guarantees fish in the frying pan. Because you are outside of your usual structures, traveling includes some stresses – making connections, cancelled flights, getting lost, not understanding the language or customs, long hours on the road, not allowing enough time for packing, etc. Younger children have a particularly difficult time with the loss of their familiar routines. Remember that infant screaming on the plane or that dad threatening Junior with annihilation if he hears one more complaint?

On a recent trip I came across the most desperately miserable couple I have ever seen. She drank herself into a stupor. He criticized. They fought. This was a tragedy, especially given the circumstances. A completely ruined rest opportunity. Well, I will not dwell on these unfortunates. I will focus on a couple that was more successful.

Lori, my wife, and I were celebrating our 30th anniversary with three days in Rome and then a ten day cruise around the Mediterranean Sea. What follows are some excerpts from my journal.

ക   ക   ക

The Innocents Abroad

Rome, Italy—Day 1

The native language here appears to be Italian, but everyone speaks to us in English. I suppose they think that we are too dumb to understand Italian, which is true.

Before I describe any more first impressions, I must tell you of my pre-first impression. It concerns pickpockets. It seemed that nearly everyone I told about our plans for this trip warned me about these masters of the sleight of hand. This one had his camera removed from his carry bag. That one had his back pocket sliced with a razor and his wallet lifted. *They worked in pairs. One distracted me while the other went through the bag. I never felt a thing!* Everyone seemed to have a story about these clever thieves. I envisioned scenes from *Oliver Twist*—the Artful Dodger, Fagin, and the rich guy with the gold watch or fat wallet, ripe for the picking. I suspect that my role is to be the rich guy in this drama. Perhaps it is my active imagination, but I fully expect to feel only the slightest of nudges in some crowded plaza and then discover that I have been striped to my underwear. I fear the pickpockets.

So I have taken precautions. The main one is that I don't carry anything worth stealing. The second one is that I hide my few worthless valuables in my special shirt that has numerous secret security pockets. These are fool proof. In fact, at this moment I cannot find my driver's license and a fifty Euro note that I hid in one of those pockets earlier. Hopefully I can find them tomorrow after I've gotten some sleep. Anyway, I will keep you informed on the efforts of the pickpockets and my attempts to thwart them.

I will rely upon Lori to provide a more detailed account of our travels. I prefer to focus on little details and anecdotes that have interested and amused me, such as happened at the little restaurant we ate at tonight.

Waitress: "Would you like some fish?"

I'm thinking that I would very much like some fish. I love fish. Then I remembered my bride. She hates fish, especially the smell of fish. Then I remembered that this was our anniversary trip and that I love Lori *more* than fish. So, selflessly, I replied: "No thank you."

The waitress disappears into kitchen, which was nearby. We hear that she is accosted by the head waiter. There are some sharp exchanges in Italian. (Italian must be the spoken language in private settings.) The waiter appears and says, "You must try the fish. Rome is famous for its fish."

He darts back into the kitchen and in an instant returns bearing a platter with four large fish and a crab. He moves the platter under our noses and describes each fish—this is a sea bass, etc. They were very beautiful fish, very beautiful. At last he comes to the crab. "The crab is alive." He nudges it. I detect no movement. "Well, maybe asleep," he says.

"I'll have the crab," said I. And a very tasty sleeping crab it was.

Rome—Day 2

It rained today and the umbrella salesmen suddenly appeared, like earthworms when the ground gets saturated. The umbrella salesmen were everywhere. They were aggressive too. They tried to sell umbrellas to us…and we already each had one.

Now to the important point. I thought that the pickpockets had gotten to me today. I discovered that the zippered pocket in my pants—where I had stashed some cash—was open. Uh-oh! Sure enough a five Euro note was gone! Fortunately the big money, a fifty Euro note, was in the security pocket inside of the zippered pocket. They had not gotten that.

Then I thought, "Did I really have a five Euro note in my zippered pocket?" I bought a coffee cup and a scarf. I may have spent the five Euros on those. In any case, perhaps the pickpockets are less skillful than I thought. My esteem for their tradecraft is falling.

I bought the scarf because Italian men wear them and look really cool. I'm not concerned about looking cool, but I am trying to trick someone into speaking Italian to me.

Rome—Day 3

The first thing is that I definitely noticed that money was missing from my pocket today—not only from the zippered pocket but from the security pocket inside the zippered pocket. I assumed it was the pickpockets, of course. But perhaps not. A meal here. A cup of coffee there. A tour. A gift. It adds up. Still, could I have spent so much? Hmmm. Maybe.

Secondarily, I noticed a large number of news trucks and reporters as we approached the Vatican this morning. We were suspicious at first but then assumed that the Vatican always gets a lot of attention. We then toured the Vatican museums, the Sistine Chapel and Saint Peter's Basilica—a three-hour tour. While in the Sistine Chapel, our guide mentioned something about setting it up for a conclave in a couple weeks. That seemed to have some significant, but I could not place it.

As we were leaving the Vatican we again noticed all of the news reporters. There seemed to be more of them. A hawker approached and tried to sell us a tour. I explained that we had just been on the tour. Then I said, "Could I ask you a question?" "Sure," he replied. "Is something going on around here?" "Yes. The Pope resigned last night. It has been 600 years since a Pope has resigned." I thanked the hawker for enlightening us with this bit of news. And I am thankful that we were not caught in a man-on-the-street interview without knowing it. I think that could have bought us our fifteen minutes of fame. Headline: Dumb Americans at Vatican Unaware of Pope Resignation.

Rome/Cruise Ship—Day 4

Today I proved my fluency in Italian. Here is how it happened. We were standing on a street corner and an old man pulls up next to us on a scooter. He starts rattling off some question or comment in Italian. It was my scarf that fooled him, no doubt. He pauses for a response. I calmly look him in the eye and said, "No Italiano," in Italian. He looks at me. I look at him. There is a deep understanding between us. He nods and drives on.

Most importantly, I paid close attention to exactly how many Euros I had in my pockets today. I had exactly the right amount of cash at the end of the day, so I am sure that I escaped the trickery of the pickpockets. I am feeling really good about my security measures. No major loses.

Tomorrow is a down day. All of the Euros are in a little safe in our cabin. Then it will be Red Alert time for five days with ports of call in Greece and Turkey. I thought the Italian pickpockets would be the worst. Apparently I was misled. They have proved to be a disappointment. But I have high hopes for the Greeks and Turks, especially the Greeks since they are so desperate.

Izmir and Ephesus, Turkey—Day 8

I was last in Ephesus thirty-four years ago. It is much improved since then. I thought the concept behind ruins was that they got worse over time. Apparently this is not the case. I suspect that if I was able to revisit Ephesus five-hundred years from now, it would again be a pristine ancient Roman city and the Apostle Paul himself would be preaching the Gospel in the streets.

Ephesus is the third great ancient city that we have visited so far—Rome, Athens, Ephesus. Each of them has awed us with their beauty and wealth, although we see the shadow of what they were. Like creation we can only imagine the wonder before decay. But here is the greater wonder—the simple and foolish Gospel transformed many in these cities. These chosen repenters turned away from their false gods and proud philosophies to the One who rose from the dead, who will judge all men, and who eternally saves those who believe in humbling faith. Is our day so different? No, it is not.

We first experienced bartering with Turkish merchants today. They are persistent. The opening price is at least twice too high. To be respectable you must offer half or less. Even if you make no offer at all, the price comes down. Today was just a warm-up for the Grand Bazaar in Istanbul. I shall have my treasures at good prices! Well…good prices to me. I have little hope of out bargaining a Turk. Amateurs do not beat top-ranked professionals. The Turks have a few thousand years of experience in the trading arts. I have shopped at Walmart.

Lastly, the Turkish pickpockets failed today, like all of the others. But this was not a true test. We were on a tour. Every tour is very tightly controlled. We are like sheep herded and guarded by sheep dogs. The wolves cannot get to us. But for the next two days we will be on our own in a city of sixteen million. No sheep dogs. Game on!

Istanbul, Turkey—Days 9 & 10

At the famous Blue Mosque an Imam was preaching in English as all of us tourists gawked at the magnificence of the structure. He said, "Jesus is not the Son of God. Jesus is a prophet of God." Although this is blasphemy, it is refreshing to hear false religion straight out, without a head fake. We are more familiar with unbelief hiding behind the supposed screen of "science." These Muslims will have none of that nonsense. They want a clean fight. Either Jesus is the Son of God or he is not. That is the issue. Eternity hangs on the answer.

Istanbul has been the best opportunity for the pickpockets to strike. We decided to take a long unnecessary tram ride…because of a little confusion over directions and maps. We were literally cheek by jowl with the natives—packed together like sardines—all of the way to our destination to nowhere and back again. Here we were most vulnerable, pressed tightly on every side. There was even an announcement in English on the tram that said, "Be careful of larceny." Larceny is the English translation of the Turkish word for pickpockets. And yet they failed again.

Well, I'm beginning to think that these pickpockets are overblown. They must have gained renown and legendary status from careless tourists who perhaps have left a camera on a park bench or who dropped some bills when they were pulling out a hanky. Here was born the mythology of the pickpockets. *I never felt a thing. They are so clever! They work in teams.* But now that I have stressed the theory to the uttermost, I declare it false. Pickpockets? I think not.

However, this does not mean that your money will not disappear. I was the victim of a master of this craft. Here is how it happened. We were walking down a sidewalk. A young man, twenty something, with a shoeshine kit approached from the opposite direction. About ten feet away his shoe brush fell to the ground unnoticed—it seemed—by him. I said, "Stop!" and pointed to the brush. He was very grateful and wanted to shine my shoes. "Please, please!" I replied, "No thank you." He insisted. I assumed that this was his way of showing gratitude, so I allowed him to clean my shoes.

I was wearing my beat-up old hiking shoes. Cleaning makes no impression upon them. Nevertheless he scrubbed away. The water he sprayed penetrated the mesh and soaked my toes. He asked me where we were from, a common question to tourists. He asked if we had children. He told us that he is married and his wife is soon expecting.

I congratulated him. He explained that the hospital bill will be very expensive. When he was done soaking my toes he looked at Lori's shoes and asked, "The lady?" I said, "No thank you." Things were wrapping up. I offered him two Turkish lira for his unneeded services. He wanted "paper" money not coinage. He wanted euros not lira. "For my wife!" Uh-huh. Understanding slowly began to dawn upon me. After more haggling I say that four lira is all that I would give. He finally takes it after much complaining.

This was a most unsatisfactory transaction, but I learned something. When you travel don't worry about pickpockets. Beware of the shoeshine men.

ço   ço   ço

I hope you found this glimpse into my travels entertaining and restful. I could share more, but I risk becoming a bore. More importantly, publishing my additional commentary on the cultures and people we experienced may invite unwanted legal actions and imperil international relations. So I had best keep certain things to myself.

Regardless of whether or not you enjoyed my nonsense, the main purpose of this travelogue was to demonstrate how to concentrate on traveling. I was completely engaged in the venture and, because of it, I was very refreshed. If you are to derive the full benefit of traveling, you must learn to do the same.

The Adventure Right Up the Road

While I recommend visiting other countries and exotic cultures, travel rest can be obtained much closer to home. There is one significant advantage to this approach—it is cheaper. Not all have the resources for an extended excursion overseas, but nearly everyone can afford a trip to a nearby state or across the Canadian or Mexican border.

Even better, there are undoubtedly places of interest within hours of where you live that draw people from around the world. Have you explored them? Think about this, if people travel thousands of miles to visit these places, don't you think they are worthy of your attention? If you are hungry, there is no need to drive to a restaurant in the next city when there is a delicious meal on the table right in front of you.

And there is another advantage. At popular nearby travel

destinations foreigners are coming to you. They are very kindly saving you the expense of going to see them. Make the most of the opportunity and strike up a conversation. When I travel the most interesting and rewarding experiences are when I interact with the natives. I appreciate these exchanges very much…shoeshine men being the exception. I expect that many if not most travelers would be delighted to talk with the natives here, which are you.

So seize the day! Not only will this enrich your local travels, but you will be a good representative for our country. Along this last line, I recommend giving a conversational foreigner ten or twenty bucks along with your thanks that he has saved you so much money. I have never actually done this, but it seems like a good idea.

If you cannot spare ten or twenty bucks, just talk to the Americans that you bump into. Some of them—Californians or Northeasterners, for example—are just as exotic as foreigners. But even if they are from more normal places, everyone is interesting in their own way. Everyone has a story, a vocation, and probably some connection to a place you have been or even a person you know. When traveling you have an excuse to freely talk with others. "I'm a rube from Colorado. Gee-whiz is New York City always so busy!" This type of comment will usually draw a response, which is the point.

Swimming Pools and Fast Food

A word to parents with young children. Some of you think that your children will be greatly enriched by experiencing different locals and cultures at a tender age. Question: Did you also think that they would turn out to be geniuses if you played classical music when they were in the womb? Both of these expectations have about an equal chance of success.

My traveling experience with my own children is that the foremost interests in their barely formed brains were: 1) Does the hotel have a swimming pool, and 2) which fast food restaurant are we eating at next? Scenery, attractions and conversations ranked somewhat lower down the list and were rememberable only if some personally traumatic event occurred in connection with them. In other words, it does not matter much where you take little kids.

This leads to the next point. Big trips expend more wealth than little trips. Most families with young children have little wealth. Rather than shelling out mega bucks for an eco-tour in West Bengal, perhaps a modest trip to the Grand Canyon and paying down your mortgage faster is a more appropriate course. If you pay off that mortgage, you will be able to afford more distant travels when your kids will be old enough to appreciate the experience.

Better yet, we have recently learned that family vacations are much less expensive when the kids do not participate at all. Our two daughters are now married and our son is on his own. This development did wonders for our travel plans. Here is the math: two travel for less than five. What a pleasant surprise!

A Threefold Benefit

Traveling can be divided into three phases—planning, being there, and re-living. Each phase should provide rest. I will cover them one at a time.

Planning is the first phase of traveling. I'm not talking about the mechanics of traveling – reservations, passports, etc. – but rather the process of deciding where you want to go and what you will be doing when you get there. Consider this an important part of the traveling experience. If you are an excellent traveler, you should spend as much or even more time in this phase than the actual traveling itself. How? By reading books, watching videos, or exploring information on the internet. This is great fun. Plan as much as you can with your fellow travelers or at least share what you have learned with them. The more you know, the more you are prepared to experience. Plus good planning builds excitement and anticipation for the trip.

Being There—or your actual travel experience—is the second phase. I have touched on this already, but let me emphasize one thing. Wherever you are, be all there. Leave your work and gizmos behind. If you are going to be focused on these, you might as well stay at home and save your money. There is no reason to be physically standing in the Grand Bazaar in Istanbul if you are immersed in the virtual world of your gizmo.

An important but often overlooked aspect of the traveling phase is forming your memories properly. You must mentally tie them down if you want to keep them. If you don't, they will be washed overboard in all the excitement. How can you form lasting memories? Simply talk about what has happened. Replay the day at dinner or before bed. *What was your favorite thing today? I can't get over that shoeshine guy! Don't tell anyone that we didn't know that the Pope resigned."*

As intuitive as this is, you often neglect it because you try to do too much while traveling. You don't take time to contemplate what you have experienced because you think that you will miss out on experiencing something else. So you rush from one thing to the next from morning till night until you fall exhausted into bed. It all becomes a blur, like pictures taken with a moving camera. The memories never form properly because you have not paused to focus on them. The experiences are indistinct, blurred, and are soon discarded by the mind.

Along this line, I recommend keeping a journal. The process of writing is the best aid to retaining memories. By writing you think through all that you have seen, touched, tasted, smelled and heard. You select and then begin to shape what was notable or important or funny or unusual. As your thoughts take form, you choose words and phrases and sentences and paragraphs to describe them. In other words, you are concentrating on your travel. You are also making memories that you will keep all of your life.

The Gift that Keeps on Giving

This brings me to the final phase of traveling. *Re-Living* your travel experiences. This is the gift of rest that keeps on giving. It is a cold spring of rest that you can drink from again and again.

In my bag of life stories I have found that a disproportionate number come from my travels. Given the relatively small amount of time I have spent traveling, this is significant. Traveling—and other notable rest experiences—push aside all that is done by habit and routine and take the most prominent place in my memory. There is a reason for this. I love to think about them. And every time I think about them, I am refreshed from my work, which is what I need, which is why I am thinking about them in the first place. I expect that your experience is similar.

These memories are not only important to you individually. Most of your best stories are of experiences you had not alone but with others, that is, of shared rest. They are the events that bind you together by common cord. This is why these stories get pulled out of the bag again and again at family reunions or when you get together with old friends. They reveal relationship, of who you are to each other, of the closeness you formed. And when you want someone new to know who you are, you tell these stories to them.

And like all good stories, they improve with age.

Pack Your Bags

So give attention to traveling. Start planning your next trip. It will be a strong dose of rest, deeply rejuvenating.

CHAPTER TWENTY-SIX

Roughing It

I recently backpacked the famed Four Pass Loop near Aspen, Colorado. Three days, twenty-six miles, four mountain passes each at an altitude of about 12,500 feet. Here was some of the most spectacularly dramatic scenery I have ever seen. Here was also one of the more difficult hikes I have ever undertaken. Three days, twenty-six miles, four passes. I had trouble. I lost eight pounds. It was the four passes that got me.

You see, I get altitude sickness. I throw up. I can't eat. I can't drink. The higher I go, the slower I move. My breathing becomes labored, like an accident victim with a sucking chest wound. I struggle, like Klondike prospectors a century ago who carried a ton of supplies on their backs up the Chilkoot Pass. *Slowly, slowly, one baby step after another. One more step. One more.* It helped me to focus on the moment. I knew I could take one more step. If I had thought about how much farther I had to go, I would have faltered or had a psychological breakdown or just started crying. No, that last one would not have happened. I was dehydrated and my eyes were all dried out.

Nevertheless, here was refreshment.

Oh, come on! You can't be serious! Where to begin? I'll start with the sheer foolishness of it. Why are you—a middle age…er…upper middle age man— putting yourself in such a situation. Don't you know your limits? Is this your version of self-denial? You are an ascetic after all—torturing yourself like that. Was this penance for your excessive "resting?"

No, neither asceticism nor penance. I did not deliberately seek such suffering. I knew that I would be near the limit of my altitude tolerance, but with the level of exertion involved, I was closer to the edge than I expected. A little too close.

But there is no need to let a fly spoil the whole bowl of soup.

Altitude Adjustment

Sometimes, perhaps most times, things do not turn out the way you anticipated they would. This is as true for your rest experiences as for anything else. Does this mean the experience is ruined? No, it just means that it is different. Although I was in some physical discomfort during the Four Pass Loop, I could appreciate the beautiful scenery and praise the Creator for it. And I was in fine company and enjoyed the fellowship. I did not cherish the sickness and exhaustion, but I could accept it, especially since it was wrapped in these other delights. This was a package deal like most other things in life.

That could not possibly have been any fun! Admit it! Why can't you admit it?

Was the hike *fun*? Hmmm. Fun is not the word I would use. I would use descriptives such as *stretching*, *enriching* and *satisfying*. There is a place for fun in your rest bucket—entertainments, amusements, frivolities—but it is shallow water. Good deep rest is more demanding. The Four Pass Loop demanded everything I had. The return was well worth the cost.

This was not the first backpacking trip with some discomfort. I have a history in this area of probing my physical limits.

The Twenty Miler

I joined the Boy Scouts when I was twelve years old. The program immediately struck a chord with me. I loved scouting, all the way to Eagle Scout and Order of the Arrow lodge chief. I was all in.

One distinction of my troop was that we went backpacking every month. And so began my first serious, intensive rest activity. I have few memories of all those long boring years of school incarceration, but I can remember just about everything that happened while backpacking. School was my work. Backpacking provided rest from my work. I did not think in those terms back then, of course. I just liked backpacking. Something interesting always seemed to happen.

My first expedition was a three and a half mile trek. It seemed like twenty miles. Backpacking was hard! It is especially difficult when you are a tiny little runt and are carrying all of your equipment and food in an official Boy Scout rucksack, which is basically a canvas bag with shoulder straps, instead of a framed pack. But when we reached our campsite I soon recovered from the strain and discovered many other new and interesting occupations, such as latrine digging, fire building and snipe hunting. Here was a whole new world of adventure.

After a few more backpacking trips our scoutmaster considered us to be battle-hardened veterans and ready for a greater challenge. The challenge turned about to be a twenty mile hike—not a hike that felt like twenty miles, but actually twenty miles…through the wilderness…through mud and snow. In case of trouble, we took a full complement of equipment and food in our packs. Well…I did not have a pack. I still had the rucksack. And one more thing. This was a one-day hike.

Sure it was.

I would not believe it either if it were not true. Our scoutmaster fell while we were climbing down a canyon wall and wrenched his hip. Then we had to carry his stuff. The canyon had about a foot and a half of snow in the bottom of it. We hiked and hiked and hiked, until the sun went down. Then we kept going. I remember trudging along at 11 p.m., looking up at the stars, whimpering, tears running down my cheeks. I was too tired to be ashamed of them. Besides, no one could see them anyway. That was the hardest day of my life.

The hardest day of my children's lives occurred thirty-five years later on another backpacking expedition. It was the first day of our hike across the Grand Canyon. Rim to rim. Reservations were required for the campsites. I requested three campsites, but the reservations we received only provided two. This meant that we had to hike all the way to the bottom of the canyon on the first day. Fourteen miles. It was a long day, very long. It was hot as the blue blazes. Tough, very tough.

There is definitely something wrong with you. And your poor children!

There is something in the human spirit that finds refreshment in a challenge. The greater the challenge, the greater the refreshment. Would you rather be an eagle or a slug? I need the heights now and again. As for the children, there was no permanent physical damage.

Be Prepared

Like other activities I have discussed, there is much more rest in backpacking than just being on the trail. In the last chapter I mentioned the three phases of traveling—planning, being there and reliving.

While writing this, I have been enjoying the reliving phase of some of my exploits. All three of the phases apply to backpacking, of course, but the planning phase has a distinction. Specialized equipment is required.

Because you must carry everything, you do not want to pack too much. Because you only have what you carry, you do not want to pack too little. The novice backpacker usually does both – he carries too much and too little. He straps on a folding chair but forgets the toilet paper. He soon discovers that he did not really need the chair.

There is an art to packing just the right equipment. Perfecting the art requires time and attention. You learn from your mistakes. You learn from others. You learn from books and magazines and websites and seminars. You learn by going to sporting goods stores and browsing through the backpacking equipment. And you find yourself talking about all of this with others who share the same interest.

In addition to equipment, there is the art of eating. *What do I like? How do I prepare it? Should I try something new? What is the right amount? How will the conditions effect my appetite?* There is the study of location. *Where should I go? How many days? How far each day? What is the vertical ascent and descent? Is there water? What will the temperature and weather be? Are there bears in the area?*

Finally, there is the craft of wilderness living. *Where do I place the tent? How do I keep dry? How do I keep warm? How do I keep cool? How do I keep the bears from eating my food? How do I prepare for emergencies? How do I treat blisters? How do I make a fire after rain? How do I put my boots on when they are frozen stiff?*

There is much to learn and do. Unless you are a wilderness guide, all of it is change from work. All of it requires concentration. All of it is a gift from God. All of it is rest.

Cousins and Cabins

Backpacking has three cousins—hunting, which is backpacking with meat (hopefully), and hiking, which is backpacking without the pack, and camping, which is backpacking without the hike. Each of these takes place in the great outdoors, utilizes unique equipment, and requires specialized knowledge.

There are many other rest activities that share some or all of these characteristics. I chose my favorite so that I could tell a few stories.

Your own favorite should have come to mind. If you do not have a favorite activity along these lines, perhaps it is time to develop one.

A cabin is a good place to begin. A cabin is just like backpacking, except without the hiking and packing and camping features. It does have some specialized equipment—comfy overstuffed chairs, a toasty woodstove and queen-size beds. And you don't have to be crazy.

CHAPTER TWENTY-SEVEN

The Cabin

People know that I am a writer and often remark that my cabin must be the perfect place to write. They imagine me pecking away at the keyboard with a crackling fire in the fireplace, a pleasant aroma of coffee in the air, a magnificent view out of every window, and, to cool my brain and refresh my imagination, taking a walk in the quiet grandeur. I can picture this idyllic scene myself. The thing is, I have never written a word at the cabin and I don't intend to.

Holy Places

The cabin is holy. I am not saying that the cabin is holy in the same sense that God is holy or that Christians are to reflect his moral excellence and purity. I am using the term is the general sense of being "set apart," of being separated from one thing so as to be dedicated to another. The cabin is separated from work and dedicated to rest. So, since writing is work for me, and I cannot rest while working, I do not write at the cabin.

I hope that at this point in the book you realize that you need to be intentional about your rest. If you are not, you will not rest well. Setting apart a specific place—actually places—for rest is an important aspect of becoming intentional about rest. Establishing rest places is a necessary part of building good rest structure in your life.

You do not require a cabin for this, of course. Almost anywhere may be a place of rest. Many public places are specifically designed for rest, such as the theater, the sports stadium, the club house, the gym, the park. There are also private places at hand where you take rest. These may be the kitchen table where you have devotions in the early quiet of the morning, the overstuffed chair for evening reading, the deck or porch, the garage, the craft room, the garden.

My mother remembers her father, my grandfather, coming home from work and sitting in the stairwell. My grandfather was a lawyer and held a position of some responsibility. What was he doing in the stairwell? He watched the cars go by. This was mentioned to me once in passing years ago, but I remembered it. At first I thought my grandfather was perhaps a little odd or even eccentric. But now I think that I understand why he was sitting in the stairwell. He was resting. He was recovering from work. The stairwell was a holy place for him.

These examples—the stairwell, the kitchen table, the park—are locations for the daily or weekly practice of rest. But what about when you require a deeper and longer rest? Where can you go when you need to drink a gallon of rest, not just take regular sips? As I have written, there are many ways to satisfy this thirst. For me, the primary way is to go to the cabin.

I assumed that the cabin would be a good rest place before I bought it. I assumed but I did not really know, just as there is no way to really know the temperature of the water until you jump into the creek. I had to buy the cabin and settle in for a while to find out. I am pleased to say that the experiment has been successful—not only for me but for my family and our friends. In fact, my children gave me a gift for the cabin. It is a wood sign that reads:

Rest and Give Thanks

That sign reminds me—and every other visitor—the purpose of the cabin. It is a place to receive and enjoy deep rest. It is a place to give thanks to God for his gracious gift of rest.

Familiarity Breeds Content

There is a kind of refreshment that comes with doing something new and different. That is why I recommend travel. But there is something special about a familiar place, a place soaked in your own memories. Your history hangs around in the decorations and furniture and landscape. You do not need to explore and discover this place because it is *your* place. All you have to do is settle back in. It is comfortable like a favorite sweater.

This is my experience at the cabin and I am not alone. I am surprised when I tell others about my cabin how big smiles break across many of their faces. Then suddenly, even though they are still looking at me, they are no longer focused on me. They see mom and dad's cabin or grandpa's cabin or Uncle Jake's cabin in their mind's eye. And they stop listening to me and start telling me their own cabin stories. I do not mind this because their stories are more interesting than mine. I've already heard mine.

There is a small cabin on the plot just below mine. I have rarely seen anyone there. However, during my last visit it was occupied by a young man named Sam. I talked to him, of course. That is what cabin neighbors do. Sam told me that his grandfather built that little cabin. Sam had spent some time growing up there. He told me that his best memory of his dad was building fires together in the fireplace. I could tell that there was a lot in that story. I hope my grandchildren have such memories.

Evacuate the City

Cabin rest begins when I pull out of my driveway. It takes about twenty minutes to drive through the city before the climb up into the mountains begins. Then it is up, up and further, further away from hustle and bustle and closer and closer to cabin life. A transition occurs—not only geographically from high prairie to mountains and from city to country, but mentally from work to rest. I set aside my work burdens during the drive.

The opposite occurs on the return trip from the cabin. About halfway home I start thinking about work. It is not as though I want to or plan to think about work. It just happens. A problem will pop into my head and I will begin to mentally work on it. *What am I going to do with Jimmy, who has attacked our contractors, alienated his co-workers, and filed grievances against everyone? How will I reprioritize projects in response to the latest budget cuts? Is it now time to initiate formal church discipline in that case of sexual sin?* These are the very issues that seemed to jump out of the car on the way to the cabin. Just like in some zombie apocalypse, they now are re-entering the vehicle on the trip home and are intruding on my consciousness.

Consciousness is the right concept here. Consciousness is the state of being aware of something. When I drive, hopefully I am conscious of the road, the traffic and the speedometer. But I have room in my braincase for more awareness. The other thoughts that fill my mind may be about any number of things. For this discussion, it is not the topic that matters. It is the category. Am I thinking about work or rest? If I am thinking about work, I am working. If I am thinking about rest, I am resting. To be a good rester, I need to be aware whether I am mentally working or resting and how I transition between the two. In other words, I need to be conscious of what I am conscious of.

(Undoubtedly thoughts about work continue to simmer in the recesses of my mind, my subconscious. This is where I want them to be. But even during the best resting times, they will sometimes boil to the surface. The question is, once I become aware of them how long will they hold my attention? A fleeting thought about work is inevitable, but dwelling on it will end my rest. When work enters my consciousness, I am learning to acknowledge the intrusion and then refocus on my rest activity. I suggest that you learn to do the same.)

So cabin travel provides a natural mental transition first to rest and then a return to work. Leaving the physical location of work facilitates entering the mental state of rest. And vice versa. This same transitioning process occurs in some other rest activities. It occurs during vacation travel. It occurs during outdoor adventures, such as camping or hiking. It occurs to some degree anytime you leave your work locations, including home, and go somewhere for rest purposes.

Solitude or Rumpus

Now that I have described the ride, I will focus on the destination. What kind of rest activities occur at the cabin? Well, all of my favorite ones. I have already sprinkled cabin anecdotes in the previous chapters. Since there would be little value in repeating a description of different types of rest activities, I will only tell how these are expressed at the cabin. Also, I will divide activities into the categories of solitary, those done alone, and communal, those done with others.

Solitary activities first. Since I am married and marriage unites two into one, I am counting the cabin time with my wife in the solitary column. Occasionally Lori or I will be at the cabin alone singly, but most times we are together. So with this qualification, of my total cabin time roughly half is solitary (with Lori) and half includes additional people (communal).

Our solitary time is best characterized as quiet and unrushed. For our time together we enjoy hiking, reading aloud, board games and listening to music. Individually, we both spend a good amount of time in devotions, reading and various projects. I am attempting to become a fisherman. They say that the pleasure is in the fishing, not necessarily the catching. I enjoy the eating part myself. However, I have adopted a philosophical outlook. The very few delicious trout I have actually landed gives me hope that my fishing pastime will become more and more culinary as I improve. Nevertheless, sitting by the lake with a line in water in the wee hours of the night or before sunrise is certainly solitary time in every sense of the word.

Communal cabin time includes others, often in significant numbers. This time is quite different from an experience of solitude. Polar opposites, you may say. Serenity is displaced with noise, bustle, activity. We enjoy campfires, hiking, climbing, shooting, Frisbee golf, lumberjacking, kayaking, games. And conversation. We have some of the best conversations at the cabin. Friendships are deepened. Family bonds are strengthened. Sometimes deep needs are expressed. When work pressure is removed we discover the person beneath the role.

The only common factor between solitary and communal times at the cabin is location. Other than that, they are different rest experiences. Different is good. You need variety in rest as you do in everything else. You also need to have expectations that are consistent with the activity. I cannot expect a weekend of contemplation if the College and Career group is joining us at the cabin. I need to brace myself for an exhilarating time of rest.

Cabinlessness

There is just something about a cabin. "Cabin" is a solely an American usage, apparently, because my Australian and Canadian friends insist on referring to my cabin as a "cottage." The Russians call cabins "dachas." New Zealanders use the term "bach." The Swedish word is "fritidshus" or "stuga." I am sure that other nationalities and cultures are equally confused about the proper terminology, but the point is that the concept of a holiday home is widespread. When you observe common practice across cultures there is usually something behind it.

That would be the need for serious rest.

I don't have a cabin! You mock me! You build up all of this cabin business and I can't do it. What about me? Am I cursed to live restlessly?

Well, not everyone has a cabin. Most people do not. In fact, I have not had one for nearly all of my life. There is still hope for you, friend. You have options.

If you have the means, you can buy one for yourself. That is the most direct approach, but it is not a prudent financial one for most people. Inheritance is an affordable way to get into cabinhood, but it requires blood connections. Then there are friends. *I'll be your friend if I can use your cabin?* This is not subtle but it works on simpletons like me. I think that an empty cabin is a waste and are glad when others benefit from it. No friends with cabins? Renting is a practical option.

You may even be a person for whom—despite my best efforts—cabin rest has little appeal. The rustic simplicity of a cabin surrounded by glorious wilderness is not for you. You would prefer a hotel rated with a lot of stars near restaurants rated with lots of stars. If that is your ideal for rest, go for it!

Rest is the destination. You need to figure out how to get there.

CHAPTER TWENTY-EIGHT

Everything Else

There are many more ways to rest than my short list of favorites. Your set will not be the same as mine because you are not me. You have your own interests, skills and abilities. And you may or may not own a cabin.

Here, in no particular order, are some additional suggestions: fishing, boating, shooting, hunting, camping, cooking, grilling, baking, crochet, knitting, needlepoint, magic tricks, board games, crossword puzzles, Sudoku, jigsaw puzzles, carpentry, furniture making, antique refurbishment, collections, bird watching, four wheeling, movies, television series, painting, drawing, sculpting, eating out, theater, playing an instrument, composing songs, singing, poetry, writing, cartooning, flying drones or model airplanes, photography, astronomy, bookbinding, historical research, home decorating, scrapbooking, card making, biking, walking, weight lifting, wood chopping, whittling, garage sale shopping, house remodeling, redecorating, gardening, landscaping, hobby clubs, civic clubs, book clubs, sewing, visiting friends, sharing a meal, storytelling, Frisbee golf, park sitting, jogging, learning another language, correspondence, family reunions, holiday traditions, and car restoration.

I am sure that there are many more. What will provide refreshing change and concentration for you?

Final Thought
Something To Look Forward To

Here, at long last, is the end. Well done faithful reader. You have persevered. I commend you.

Thanks but I have one more thing to say.

What is it?

Was it really necessary to labor through all of that theology and theory before you got to the practical stuff?

Well, it was for me. I need to understand the *why* before I do the *what*. Writing this book has been a self-imposed exercise in thinking through the foundation and practice of rest. Hopefully it will prove useful to you too.

Really it is very simple. God is a working-resting God and you are made in his image. Because you are, you must rest. To rest well requires intentionality on your part, just like mastering anything else. Your rest activities must include the elements of change and concentration. You must also build daily, weekly and yearly structures of rest into your life. As a Christian, you have graciously been given both the freedom and responsibility to do this.

There is a utilitarian purpose for rest—it multiplies your work productivity. But rest is also good in and of itself. Rest is not a necessary evil. You should live for the glory of God in your rest just as you do in your work.

And one final thing. Always have something to look forward to. This may be as simple as reading a good book before bed or as involved as taking a vacation to some adventurous place. You need these activities, small and large, to provide refreshment from your work. Without rest you are a runner without a finish line ahead of you.

Rest is a reward for work. It is a cool breeze on a hot day. Rest is a blessing, a gift from God. Receive it. Give thanks for it. Honor Jesus through your rest.

Rest well, friend.

Appendix A
Your Theological Jigsaw Puzzle

It is important to clearly distinguish between the divinely inspired and illuminated *words* of the Bible and theology, which is an attempt to synthesize those words into a *logical system*. The first is God's business and the second is yours. If you fail to make this distinction, you are likely to claim divine inspiration for your theology. This will not be helpful. Humbly admit that theology is a building of your own making—or, more likely, a building that others have made and that you have moved into. Again, this is not to say that you can do without theology. You cannot because of the way you think about things.

I once fellowshipped with a group of believers that claimed that they had no theology. *We simply believe the words of the Bible. No unspiritual manmade theology for us!* This sounded good and I believed it at first. But after a while I discovered that they did indeed have a theology—one of the most complex and detailed theologies I have ever encountered. However, they did not write it down as such. They published lots of commentaries but no books on systematic theology. But there was theology aplenty in those commentaries, as well as throughout their preaching and teaching. It cannot be avoided.

Christian faithfulness does not require a mystical escape from the hard mental work of theology but rather a commitment to make good theology—theology based upon accurate, contextual interpretation of the Bible. This is a difficult and continuing task. The study of rest is one small part of that task.

I would like you to ponder this concept of theology through the use of analogy. Making theology is much like putting a jigsaw puzzle together. There is a method to it. Assembling a puzzle involves three basic steps.

The Big Picture

The first step is to conceptualize what the puzzle is about. What do all of the little pieces form? This is no mystery when it comes to puzzles. Just look at the puzzle box. Here is the big picture. *Ah-ha! It is a scene about a ship on the high seas, a quilting circle, or a cabin in the mountains.* The cabin, of course, is an ever popular and most pleasant puzzle motif.

What is the overall picture that the Bible forms? What is it all about? You do not have to guess. Jesus tells you.

> And beginning with Moses and all the Prophets, he interpreted to them in all the Scriptures the things concerning himself.
>
> Luke 24:27

Jesus says that the Bible is all about him. He is the scene. He is the picture on the box. But this picture is not a simplistic one. You cannot just glance at it and master the message. It is not a bumper sticker that says, "Jesus Saves!" No. This is an epic picture of redemption. Although centered on the Redeemer, all kinds of things are happening in the picture—characters, history, poetry, apocalypse. There is depth and complexity here and much to contemplate and study. Nevertheless, whether you are reading the Bible for the first time or the ten thousandth time, you should always keep this overall idea in mind.

Some argue that this approach is exactly backwards. They contend that forming the big picture should be the last step. First, they say, you must master the details of Scripture—the words, the verses, the books—and then form conclusions. You must build from the bottom up, inductively, not from the top down, deductively. I like this in theory and wish that it were so. But I am not describing theory but practice. You interpret the details of the Bible in light of your conception of the big picture. By the way, this is generally the way people think about things, whether they label the big picture as theology, worldview or philosophy. An overall assumption or presupposition concerning the subject shapes how the details are interpreted.

The Pieces

Enough of the picture. It is time to put the pieces together. You do this in two additional steps.

The next or second step of puzzle making is to look for distinctive elements—themes—in the picture. What parts of the scene immediately draw your eye? (Let us return to the beloved cabin motif.) There is the cabin itself—log siding with green trim. There is bluish smoke rising from the chimney. There is a towering rock outcropping.

These features draw your attention because their unique colors and shapes make them stand out. You can quickly find these puzzle pieces and put them together. These are the easiest sections of the puzzle.

In the same way, the major themes of the Bible are quickest for you to grasp and understand. That is because they are explained clearly and extensively. What are the major themes? At the highest level, these can be described as created order, Old Covenant, New Covenant, and re-creation. A well-formulated theology should be based upon an understanding of these most significant teachings.

The third step to complete the puzzle is more difficult. You still have all of those "background" pieces lying around—the trees, the field, the sky—that look so similar to one another. You save these pieces until last because they are the hardest to fit in. What helps with these is to have much of the puzzle completed in step two.

You follow the same approach in theology. After you have formulated an understanding of the major themes of the Bible, you fit the smaller details and connecting pieces around these themes. The work you have already completed provides a framework and context for what remains. There are many lesser themes in Scripture, teachings that are not explained extensively. Angels and demons are examples of these. And so is rest. When your theology is accurate, these pieces will fit right into the major biblical themes.

The Wrong Picture!

Although jigsaw puzzles fit together in these three steps, theology often does not. Puzzles fit together in three steps because the picture on the box is the picture that the pieces form. This is not necessarily so with theology. The text of Scripture does not always form the picture you have in mind. (Remember that you conceptualized the picture before we started putting the pieces together.) There is a fourth step for theology and it is the most difficult of all. In order to continue with the puzzle analogy, a little more imagination is required.

Imagine that the puzzle was put in the wrong box at the puzzle factory. The picture on the box and the puzzle in the box do not match. The puzzle makers did not do this deliberately, they just got careless. You see, this particular factory makes various puzzles of the beloved cabin motif. The puzzle pictures are all similar in composition but not exactly the same.

The trouble starts when you begin to work on the puzzle. The pieces do not all fit together the way you think they should because of your understanding of the big picture. Some of the pieces do not seem to fit into the picture at all. You get frustrated, confused and may even try to force pieces together. The problem is not with the puzzle, of course. It is with the picture. You are looking at the wrong picture!

Once you get over the shock of this discovery, you look again at all the puzzle pieces spread across the puzzle board. The pieces that form the cabin are easy to spot, and you pick them out and assemble them. Eureka! The cabin in this puzzle is different from the one pictured on the box. It is time to take action.

> Dear Beloved Cabin Motif Puzzle Factory,
> I am returning this puzzle box to you. After much agonizing, I have discovered that it is the wrong box for my puzzle. My puzzle forms a picture of a cabin with a brown metal roof. The picture on the box is of a cabin with a red metal roof. This is obviously inconsistent. Please provide the correct box so that I can complete the puzzle. Thank you for your consideration.
> P.S. A little more attention to detail will save your customers a lot of grief.
> A. Buding Theologian

Note that the mismatch between the puzzle and the picture forced you to reverse your usual method. Since you could not proceed deductively, from the picture to the pieces, you had to proceed inductively, from the pieces to the picture. This is exactly what the critics of step one said should have happened in the first place. Note also that the letter writer wants the new box so that he can "complete the puzzle." Having assembled the cabin pieces inductively, he has no desire to continue this approach to puzzle work. He wants the picture to help him put the rest of the puzzle together. Hopefully he will get the right box with the right picture this time.

The Pain of Re-Drawing

If you discover that your theological picture is inaccurate in some detail, correcting it will be far more difficult than writing to a puzzle factory. You usually have a lot invested in your picture. For one thing, your church. While the major theological boundaries of historic Christian orthodoxy are broad enough to encompass different perspectives, you should support the particular doctrinal viewpoint of the church you attend. That is, you should be in agreement, be generally of one mind, within the fellowship of a local body. The picture presented here may not be accepted. A change to your theological picture may also impact you in other personal ways. Perhaps you have been taught a certain theology since childhood. This picture forms your understanding of life and a change to this will touch you and your family deeply.

This is all to point out that my theology of rest may be unsettling to you.

Why stir the pot then? Because poor theology will result in practical confusion. And confusion is the devil's playground. There is danger in misunderstanding rest—danger of having a disconnect between what you think and what you experience.

I am realistic enough to realize that this book will not be warmly received by everyone. If this is the case for you, I only hope to provoke you to seriously study the Scriptures. That is what I have attempted to do.

ACKNOWLEDGMENTS

Many thanks to my friends who have reviewed this manuscript and suggested many improvements both in content and style, as well as pointing out the obvious errors and unintentionally offensive remarks—Kok Yiang Khew, Chris Powell, Ian McIntosh, Chuck and Ellen Graham, Nate Mirza, Eric Smith, Tyler Curtis, Dwight Brown, Doug Goodin, Erik Van Os and Scott Shannon.

And, as I have repeatedly promised, my gratitude to all of the "Little People" of Front Range Alliance Church who have endured many classes—some of which were half-baked—over the years I was writing about rest. Thank you for your patience and especially for your interaction, which has shaped this material. You deserve much credit…and I will graciously accept it for you.

ABOUT THE AUTHOR

Robert L. Franck is an unexceptional man by all measures.
Like many others, he is a husband, a father and a grandfather. He
earns his bread the conventional way—by working for a salary. He
also serves as an elder in his church. If there is anything notable
about him it is that he writes more slowly than anyone else on earth.

And he has a nice little cabin.

୨ଚ   ୨ଚ   ୨ଚ

Also by the author:

The Pursuit of Common Man:
A Tale of Christianity and Common American Culture

The Streets of Glory (A Novel)

୨ଚ   ୨ଚ   ୨ଚ

For a free discussion guide to this book and additional writings, visit
his website at **www.slowthoughts.com**.

CPSIA information can be obtained
at www.ICGtesting.com
Printed in the USA
FSHW012019121218
54444FS